The New York Times
BOOK OF
NATURAL DISASTERS

Other books in the series:

The New York Times Book of Birds
The New York Times Book of Fossils and Evolution
The New York Times Book of Archeology

The New York Times

BOOK OF

NATURAL DISASTERS

EDITED BY
NICHOLAS WADE

THE LYONS PRESS
GUILFORD, CONNECTICUT
An imprint of The Globe Pequot Press

Contents

Introduction

When geologists lecture about geological change—all those raised seabeds, basaltic floodplains, eroded mountain ranges—they are usually referring to events that happened millions of years ago. But the violent energies that remold the Earth's surface have not subsided. They labor so slowly that it takes thousands of years for their effects to become apparent. But they are still as much at work today as at any time in the geological past.

Nature is often said to be tamed, but natural disasters kill about a million people around the world every decade, and leave millions more homeless. There is nothing tamed or tamable about tornadoes, hurricanes, volcanoes, earthquakes or tsunamis. Drawing on energy from the sun or the Earth's residual heat, these titanic forces landscape the planet according to their random design. There is no refuge or protection against them except to get out of their way.

And these are just the junior category of natural disasters. The worse kind no one can avoid, but fortunately they strike on a timescale of thousands of millions of years. One is global climate change. The other is the impact of large asteroids or comets.

The world's climate has been much warmer than it is now—for example, during much of the age of the dinosaurs that ended 65 million years ago. It has also been much colder during the great ices that have punctuated the world's climatic history and the during the last of which the human species evolved to its present form.

The past 10,000 years, since the last ice age ended, seems to have been an unusually even and temperate period. It will not last forever. Maybe thousands of years hence, maybe much sooner, another great ice age will once again send the glaciers southward, locking much of North America in their silent embrace. But before that, the climate may become significantly warmer. Experts believe they can already discern the first traces of a global temperature rise caused by industrial gases accumulating in the atmosphere and trapping the sun's heat.

Climate change of any kind, whether warmer or cooler, would have wide-ranging repercussions on natural ecosystems and specifically on agriculture. A warming climate would be accompanied by a global rise in sea level that would render many coastal regions and oceanic islands uninhabitable. Although both nature and the world's economies could probably adapt well enough to a slow shift in global temperatures, a precipitous climatic change, like those that seem to have occurred often in the past, could present serious challenges.

Another kind of natural disaster that is unavoidable because of its global effects is the impact of a large comet or asteroid. These visitations seem to occur every 20 million years or so. Although the footprint of the impact may be relatively small, it injects a cloud of rock dust into the high atmosphere, where it may veil the sun for years, wreaking irreparable havoc on plants and animals throughout the world.

Depressing though this list of calamities may be, the situation is not completely hopeless. As the following articles show, a good beginning has been made on understanding the scientific principles behind many of these phenomena. Hurricanes, among the most destructive of natural disasters, can now be predicted so well that loss of life can be almost completely avoided. Property losses are another matter.

Volcanoes, earthquakes and tsunamis remain unpredictable and continue to cause enormous damage. But the first steps have been taken to curb the emission of industrial waste gases and restrain their possible influence on global climate. And telescopes are busily scanning the skies for Earth-threatening asteroids. If one is spotted, there should in principle be time to devise a space probe that will change the asteroid's course.

The following articles were written by the science staff of *The New York Times* and appeared mostly in the newspaper's science section. My colleagues and I thank Lilly Golden of the Lyons Press for the idea of assembling them in book form.

1

VOLCANOES

Volcanologists practice one of the world's most dangerous professions. They congregate around active volcanoes, recording the vibrations and vapors from the sleeping dragon, hoping to find some pattern that will let the moment of its terrible awakening be predicted. But so far volcanoes have preserved their reputation for erratic behavior, and every year volcanologists are killed or injured in pursuit of their perilous quest.

Stanley Williams, whose account is described herein, was the only survivor of the sudden eruption of the Galeras volcano in Colombia, which killed six researchers. Yet as soon as he had recovered from a fractured skull and two broken legs, he was back on the job.

Volcanologists know that the lives of thousands of people may depend upon their efforts. Around the world some 500 million people live dangerously close to volcanoes, drawn there by the flat mud plains and rich soil of previous eruptions. Of the 1,500 known volcanoes, about one third have been active within the last 400 years, meaning they are still liable to erupt again.

Unlike hurricane warnings, which are both believable and believed, warnings about volcanoes are neither. People often ignore volcanologists' advice, sometimes with impunity, sometimes not. In the movies, people outrun the sluggish flows of molten lava. In real life, the searing heat and sulfurous gases overwhelm the lungs of everyone in their path. These dragons feed from the Earth's primeval heat and are implacable destroyers.

Seriously destructive volcanoes have been quite rare, at least in the recent past. There have been four major eruptions in the last 200 years.

- The Tambora volcano in Indonesia exploded in 1815. Some 10,000 people died immediately from the ashfall and the destructive tidal wave known as a tsunami, and another 80,000 perished in the famine caused by damage to agriculture. In Europe and North America 1815 became known as the "year without a summer." Although the reason was not understood until many years later, Tambora injected into the stratosphere a long, lingering veil of dust particles that weakened sunlight around the world.

- Krakatoa, another volcano in Indonesia, exploded in 1883. Its tsunami drowned 36,000 people in the neighboring islands of Java and Sumatra. Its dust veil chilled the world's climate by half a degree centigrade for several years afterward.
- The Mount Peleé volcano in the Caribbean island of Martinique erupted in 1902, destroying the port of St. Pierre and 29,000 people.
- The most recent killer volcano was Nevada del Ruiz in Colombia. A gigantic mudflow created by the 1985 eruption wiped out the town of Armero and 25,000 people.

The volcano at Mount St. Helens in Washington State erupted in 1980. One side of the mountain exploded in a tremendous blast that felled some 10 million trees, but the loss of human life was small.

Volcanoes pose several quite distinct kinds of hazard. They can kill by the blast of their explosions, by toxic gases, by ashfalls and by streams of molten lava. One of their most deadly emanations is what geologists call pyroclastic flow, a fluidized emulsion of gas and dust. These heavy, burning clouds can move with deadly speed, traveling up to several miles per minute. Their scalding temperature ranges from 100 degrees centigrade—the boiling point of water—to seven times as hot. They burn and devastate everything in their path.

Those who may escape the direct hazards of volcanoes then face the indirect consequences of volcanic action such as avalanches, mudflows and tsunamis.

When a Volcano Turns Deadly
for Those Studying Its Moods

HIS LEGS BROKEN AND JAW wired shut, a battered survivor of one of the worst disasters in the history of scientific fieldwork has recounted from a hospital bed how six colleagues died the month before while searching for better ways to predict when volcanoes are going to blow up.

The six were killed on January 14, 1993, as they gathered chemical and gravitational clues in the cone of the Galeras volcano, stretching 13,680 feet into the cold, thin air of the Colombian Andes. The ground suddenly began to heave. With a deafening roar, the volcano exploded in a riot of incandescent boulders and lava and ash, some thrown miles high.

The blast crushed or burned to death six scientists in or near the crater. The lone survivor among the group was Dr. Stanley N. Williams, a 40-year-old volcanologist at Arizona State University who is married and the father of two small children, aged seven and four.

Dr. Williams, standing on the crater's eastern rim, watched helplessly as two colleagues inside the crater and three on the opposite rim were caught in the upheaval.

"I said to myself, 'I don't want to die. I don't want to lose my wife and kids,' " he recalled in a telephone interview from a hospital in Phoenix. "I turned and ran as fast as I could. I didn't make it very far, only about twenty meters below the rim."

His skull fractured and legs broken, Dr. Williams fought to retain consciousness while crumpled on the slope so he could watch for falling boulders, dodging them as they dropped.

The catastrophe struck as 90 scientists from 15 countries met at a conference in Pasto, Colombia, to study the Galeras volcano as part of a United Nations effort to reduce the death toll from natural disasters. The volcano had been judged likely to have a large eruption this decade and to pose a significant threat to humans.

Pasto, with a population of 300,000, lies at the foot of the volcano's eastern slope a few miles from the crater, and a total of 400,000 people live on the volcano's flanks. Galeras is today the most active of the Colombian volcanoes, having had major eruptions with lava flows in 1936 and 1945 and a number of minor ones since reawakening five years ago, including an eruption in July of 1992.

Dr. Williams led the American contingent at Pasto, which is about 375 miles southwest of Bogotá in the Andes near Ecuador. The disaster struck during a field trip by the 90 scientists to examine the volcano and collect data.

Although the absence of discernible warning underscored the primitive state of eruption forecasting, the scientists now recovering from the disaster say measurements made at the Galeras crater hold significant promise for the future. Chemical clues in vented gas and subtle shifts in the volcano's overall gravitational field, they say, may eventually give scientists a new kind of alarm system.

"They could tell us when we're getting into a dangerous period and more surveillance is needed," said Dr. John Stix, a volcanologist at the University of Montreal who helped organize the meeting.

In theory, such warnings could save many lives. However, volcanoes are fickle. They have distinct personalities and all too often show little similarity in their patterns of discontent. While Galeras exploded with no warning, Kilauea on Hawaii sent all sorts of clear signals before erupting after midnight on January 2, 1983, beginning one of the longest volcanic eruptions in recorded history.

The ground around Kilauea shook and became distended as molten rock forced its way toward the surface. Finally, after nearly 24 hours of warm-up exercises, earthquakes were replaced by rhythmic vibrations, a sign of gushing lava. Sure enough, the nighttime darkness around the volcano was lighted by a red glow.

In 1989, one year after Galeras reawakened, the Colombian government established a geologic observatory at Pasto to monitor Earth tremors, and ringed the volcano with a network of seismic sensors. It also set up stations to measure rises in ground height, which are thought to occur as magma (the molten rock that turns into lava) accumulates in reservoirs beneath a volcanic summit. Such monitoring, however, gave no warning of the recent fiery explosion.

Among the aims of the weeklong Galeras meeting, which began three days before that eruption, was to discuss bolstering such traditional methods with newer and more sensitive ones.

A day after the meeting opened, Dr. Geoff C. Brown, a geologist at the Open University in Britain, presented a paper on how infinitesimal changes in gravity around volcanoes could help reveal the upward movement of magma. When a volcano becomes distended, it moves ever so slightly, often just inches, away from the Earth's center of gravity. This produces a very small reduction in the strength of the gravitational field at the volcano that can be measured by instruments of great sensitivity.

Another stratagem discussed at the meeting was tracking changes in the composition of vented gas. As magma rises near the surface and undergoes a huge drop in pressure, dissolved gases come out of solution (like carbon dioxide bubbling out of a bottle of soda or seltzer). At first the lightest gases predominate—carbon dioxide, followed by water vapor. But if magma sits in a reservoir, getting relatively old, the rush of light gases is eventually replaced by heavier ones like sulfur dioxide and hydrogen chloride.

Thus, geochemists believe that monitoring the composition of vented gas might announce the arrival of fresh magma—and warn of increased danger of an eruption.

Both chemical and gravitational clues were being gathered during the morning field trip to Galeras on January 14. Everything went smoothly at first amid the cool fog swirling about the volcanic peak. More than a dozen scientists entered the volcano's crater to collect data, as well as some journalists and tourists.

Evacuated bottles were used to sample gases. Dr. Brown of the Open University took gravity measurements on a portable meter.

By noon or a little afterward, half the scientists had finished their work and left the crater. Four Colombians stayed—Dr. José Arles Zapata, a geochemist at the Pasto observatory; Dr. Fernando Cuenca, a geophysicist from Bogotá who had conducted a magnetic survey of the volcano; Dr. Nestor García, an industrial chemist at the National University; and Dr.

Carlos Trujillo, a community college teacher in Pasto who liked to use the volcano as a classroom.

Also remaining were Dr. Brown and Dr. Igor Menyailov, 67, a Russian scientist from the Institute of Volcanology in Petropavlovsk on the Kamchatka peninsula.

The Russian relaxed at the bottom of the crater, happy with the day's work, smoking a cigarette. "He had never been to South America before," Dr. Williams recalled. "He was excited."

Dr. Williams stood on the crater's eastern rim as the remaining scientists left or got ready to leave. "I was talking to them about what they were doing and whether they were pleased with the data," he said. "Igor stood there smoking. He was going to climb up to me."

Suddenly, the crater's floor began to lurch and the top of the volcano exploded in a frenzy of hot rocks and lava, killing six of the scientists as well as three nearby tourists.

"I heard this huge boom, and then rocks the size of televisions started falling around us," recalled Dr. Andrew McFarlane, a geologist at Florida International University who had got beyond the crater. Dr. McFarlane suffered a broken foot, bruises on his legs and badly burned hands from climbing over burning rocks.

Dr. Williams, fleeing the crater's rim, pounded by flying rocks, ran as far as he could down the volcanic slope before his broken legs gave way. He took shelter from the weakening eruption behind large rocks. After an hour, a second volcanic blast hurled aloft new boulders that he successfully dodged.

Through it all the Earth shook and rumbled, leaving geologists in the area fearful that the volcano had entered a new, more dangerous phase before a major eruption.

After some two hours on the crater's slope, Dr. Williams heard in the distance his graduate student, Marta Lucía Calvache, who is the acting director of the Pasto geologic observatory, and another woman calling out to see if anyone was alive.

The two women, atop a ridge overlooking the volcanic crater, came down with a stretcher and hauled Dr. Williams to safety. "They saved my life," he said, choking back emotion.

He was flown by helicopter from the volcano's side to a hospital in Pasto, and later transferred to one in Phoenix.

The eruption of Galeras turned out to be the largest there in five years, as measured by the height of its volcanic cloud and the release of seismic energy. But it did not pump lava down the side of the mountain, which could have resulted in a major catastrophe.

One of the tale's many twists is that several scientists from the United States Geological Survey who had planned to attend the meeting and would have probably been in the crater during its eruption were barred at the last minute by the State Department, which feared political violence linked to Colombia's drug lords.

A memorial of sorts to Dr. Brown of the Open University appeared in *Nature,* the British science journal. A paper of his, written with four other scientists, presented gravity data from the monitoring of Mount Etna in Sicily and concluded that measurements of ground waves and deformation had missed critical motions of magma near the surface.

"Only gravity changes," Dr. Brown and his colleagues wrote, "can detect the mass increase."

Why did the techniques tested at Galeras fail to warn the volcanologists of danger? Dr. Williams said there might well have been chemical clues, but these will only be apparent after the samples are processed in the United States.

The goal of the gas program, Dr. Williams added, is a portable unit that could be left near a volcanic vent to analyze gases automatically every few hours and radio the results to distant scientists. The feasibility of such a device is being investigated by Transducer Research Inc., a small company in Naperville, Illinois.

Another possible reason for the lack of warning, said Dr. Stix of the University of Montreal, is that the blasts involved no major movement of magma but simply the release of pent-up gases. If so, he said, "the volcano was less dangerous after the eruption than we had initially thought."

Dr. Williams, though shaken by the death of his colleagues, said he was ready to go back to Galeras despite the obvious dangers. He noted that volcanology was an inherently high-risk profession in which on average of one scientist dies on the job every year or so.

The Galeras disaster, he added, might have a silver lining if it focused global attention on the problems of volcanic forecasting and resulted in new funds being devoted to avoiding disasters.

"The important thing," he said, "is that people follow through with this research and make an impact."

—WILLIAM J. BROAD, February 1993

Below Yellowstone, Earth Is on the Boil

VISITORS TO YELLOWSTONE NATIONAL PARK are bedazzled by the colorful hot springs and boiling mud ponds. They scan the countryside, looking for a wolf, bison or grizzly bear and marvel at geysers spewing towers of steam and water into the air with pyrotechnic fury.

But with their eyes riveted on these surface displays of natural beauty, they remain oblivious to one of the most mind-boggling and unsettling facts that a geologist could possibly throw at a hapless tourist: if you are standing in Yellowstone Park and you could peer through the earth beneath your feet, you would see gigantic globs of partly melted rock and pressurized gas only about four and a half miles down. In effect, you would be standing on top of a molten plume that may extend to the Earth's liquid core and that may erupt to the surface at any time.

The fact that Yellowstone is a geological hot spot—a place where deep forces push through the Earth's crust and violently alter the surface—has only recently become accepted by geologists, said Nancy Hinman, a geologist at the University of Montana in Missoula who helped organize a symposium on the Yellowstone hot spot for the American Geophysical Union meeting in San Francisco. Most hot spots lie under oceans and give birth to island chains like the Hawaiian islands, Dr. Hinman said. But in Wyoming, a hot spot has created the Yellowstone caldera, a craterlike basin of a volcano, which measures 50 miles across. The last time it blew up, 600,000 years ago, ash landed in Iowa and California, making Mount St. Helens look like a hiccup.

Awed by the magnitude of earlier eruptions, geophysicists have been taking a closer look at the caldera lately, and have realized that it is still active. The caldera breathes fumes that kill plants and wildlife, rumbles and alters terrain—and it is destined to explode again, they say. They regard the caldera as a natural laboratory, a window into learning about the

Earth's composition, how convection moves the tectonic plates that form the Earth's crust, how gases behave under pressure and even for finding clues about the origin of life.

Europeans first explored Yellowstone in the early 1800s, but it was not until 25 years ago that geologists realized that it was built on a hot spot under the North American plate, and the plate was gliding over it at a rate of one inch per year, said Dr. Kenneth Pierce, a geologist at the United States Geological Survey in Denver.

But when geologists looked down the Snake River Valley that extends from Yellowstone west, they identified a string of extinct calderas running to Oregon. At least nine Yellowstonelike calderas running from Wyoming to Oregon have been discovered, Dr. Pierce said. The oldest is 16 million or 17 million years old and lies in southeastern Orgeon and northern Nevada. A caldera system near Pocatello, Idaho, called the Picabo Volcanic Field, is 10 million years old. The Heise caldera field in Idaho, about 100 miles west of Yellowstone, is five million years old.

Yellowstone, as it exists today, is less than two million years old. It was formed by three eruptions, one of which may have been the largest eruption in the planet's history, said Dr. Robert Christiansen, a geologist at the geological survey in Menlo Park, California. The explosions blasted a total of 1,600 cubic miles of material into the atmosphere. By comparison, Mount St. Helens produced about a quarter of a cubic mile of ash and lava. The first and largest eruption was Huckleberry Ridge 2.1 million years ago. Ash as much as three feet thick blanketed the Western United States. The second occurred 1.3 million years ago at Island Park. The third, at Lava Creek, happened 600,000 years ago and formed the current caldera—one that straddles the previous two.

In the textbook model of these events, a plume, or narrow chimney of magma, liquid or molten rock, travels from the core-mantle boundary of the Earth until it hits the crust, which on the continent is 20 miles to 30 miles thick. As material continues to rise, it forms a large pool of melted basalt under the crust and slowly melts the overlying rock. As the heat causes it to expand, the crust gradually thins; melted crustal rock, called rhyolite, forms bulges near the surface. These pockets of melted rock are rich in silica and release copious amounts of volatile gases that are held under high pressures. As the gases rise, cracks form around the bulges and extend down toward the magma. At this point, "the gun is cocked and loaded," Dr. Pierce said.

When the fractures encounter the magma chambers, the pressure is suddenly released, and giant fountains of 1,800-degree ash and tuff burst from the fractures. In hours, hundreds of cubic miles of material is blown out, traveling at hundreds of miles an hour, knocking down everything in its path. The roof of the caldera collapses, forming a huge depression. Magma pours into the depression, forming domes and other features. This is what visitors to Yellowstone see.

But recently, Dr. Eugene Humphreys, a geophysicist at the University of Oregon in Eugene, used seismic tomography to obtain a three-dimensional image of the Earth under a former hot spot near Pocatello. "We thought we would see the flattened plume" under the crust, Dr. Humphreys said. But instead, they found pockets of partly melted rock with especially dense, cold material to each side—and the pockets were aligned in a channel moving away from the Yellowstone hot spot.

This finding led Dr. Humphreys and his colleagues to propose a new model of how hot spots are formed and how they propagate. Magma sources that are not directly linked to the core-mantle boundary can form and rise toward the solid surface of their own accord, he said. Once this process begins, pressure is released, more melting occurs, more upwelling occurs and the system begins to propagate itself. Huge rolls of magma move like corkscrews in the direction of plate motion, drawing fresh material from below. The system is created by local processes and does not need to be driven by heat from extremely deep sources, Dr. Humphreys said.

Whatever mechanism explains it, the hot spot will continue to migrate north at a rate of 15 miles every one million years, the researchers said. Eventually it will reach Billings, Montana, lift the city 3,000 feet, drop it and move toward Hudson Bay.

Back in Yellowstone, the hot spot today is rising and falling as if breathing heavily, Dr. Pierce said. Measurements show that the caldera rose three feet from 1923 to 1985. Since then it has been dropping half an inch each year. By looking at ancient shorelines of Yellowstone's lakes and rivers that rise and fall in concert, Dr. Pierce showed that the caldera rose and fell about five times over the last 9,000 years, each time by about 25 feet.

The current swelling does not necessarily doom Yellowstone to a violent explosion soon, but the recent history of extensive volcanism, very high heat flow and earthquakes warrants "keeping an eye on the region," said Dr. Robert Smith, a geophysicist at the University of Utah in Salt Lake. Outside California, Yellowstone is the most seismically active region in the continental United States and is able to produce large earthquakes.

This activity produces the familiar landscape in the park. The silica-rich soil in the caldera is not friendly to most plants, but the lodgepole pine thrives on it, Dr. Pierce said. Miles of lodgepole pines grow in the caldera and nothing else, making it a kind of desert studded with hundreds of geysers, hot springs rings and other geothermal features.

People love geysers, Dr. Pierce said. They are formed when heat from the caldera encounters water in permeable rock and pressure builds, venting steam. Some geysers explode every few hours while others require decades between eruptions—and most are unpredictable. Steamboat Geyser erupts at intervals of five days to 50 years. Black Opal Pool in Biscuit Basin last exploded in the spring of 1925 and has since been quiet. Giant Geyser in the upper basin is springing back to life after being dormant for 40 years. It sends scalding water to a height of 185 feet or more.

The most famous of the geysers, Old Faithful, has lost its clocklike regularity. The geyser used to pop off roughly every 60 minutes, but shifting forces beneath the ground have created a bimodal pattern of eruption, said Dr. Stuart Rojstaczer, a hydrologist at Duke University in Chapel Hill, North Carolina. It tends to erupt every 40 minutes or 70 minutes, depending on the recharge rates and how rock permeability changes with steam content, he said. The short and long intervals between eruptions occur randomly.

Dr. Rojstaczer and his colleagues placed matchbox-size instruments in six geysers to monitor eruption patterns. A theory, invented primarily by Chinese seismologists about 20 years ago, holds that hydrothermal areas are sensitive zones in the crust, he said. When the Earth undergoes changes in strain just before a large earthquake, the theory goes, the behavior of the fragile geysers will change radically. The instruments are designed to test this idea, which, if true, could help scientists predict earthquakes.

In the meantime, the caldera can be deadly in other ways. New measurements show that the caldera emits as much carbon dioxide each year as 10 to 20 fossil fuel plants—enough to kill small forests or ground-dwelling animals. Much of the gas percolates through hot pools, bubbling like champagne. Such festive pools contain bacterialike organisms that thrive on hydrogen and sulfur and are among the most ancient organisms on Earth. Scientists say these exotic life-forms are found in midocean ridges and other extreme, hot environments, as well as Yellowstone—making the park a window into the planet's darkest interior secrets.

—SANDRA BLAKESLEE, April 1998

Facing the Peril of Earth's Cauldrons

PLANET EARTH IS PLANNING SOME spectacular volcanic fireworks and millions of people worldwide are going to have ringside seats.

The next show could start anytime, almost anywhere. It might be Mexico City, where a 17,000-foot volcano named Popocatepetl is spewing ash and poisonous gases toward 20 million homes; it conceivably could explode with the force of 10,000 atomic bombs.

Or it might be Vesuvius, the famed volcano that looms over Naples and surrounding Italian towns, home to 11 million people. A small volcano called Soufriere Hills is erupting now on the lush Caribbean island of Montserrat, and has already driven most of the island's people from their homes.

There are about 1,500 active volcanoes, not counting hundreds more under the oceans, and any of them could erupt at any time, said Dr. Tom Casadevall, western regional director of the United States Geological Survey in Menlo Park, California. Of the 1,500, 583 have exploded within the last 400 years, making them particularly dangerous. Each year, scientists observe 50 to 60 volcanoes in various stages of eruption, some gently extruding lava like red-hot toothpaste down hillsides, others heaving molten rock particles and noxious gases many miles up into the atmosphere.

The number of people living on the sides of volcanoes and in the valleys below has skyrocketed, said Dr. Stanley N. Williams, a volcanologist at Arizona State University in Tempe. At least 500 million people live dangerously close to volcanoes, he said. Many dwell in megacities in Asia and Latin America—Tokyo, Manila, Jakarta, Mexico City, Quito—or in cities of at least a million people. Here in the United States, the people of Seattle and Tacoma live in the shadow of Mount Rainier, a 13,000-foot volcano whose mudflows have swept through the places where the cities are situated.

People have been drawn to volcanoes for centuries because the surrounding soils are rich and old volcanic mudflows make nice flat areas for settlement, Dr. Williams said. As population rises and land gets scarcer, the problem is getting worse.

Most of the time, the people who colonize danger areas do not know any better. And the people who do know better, scientists and civil disaster officials, "are not always listened to," said Dr. Grant Heiken, a volcanologist at the Los Alamos National Laboratory in New Mexico.

For example, scientists issued a warning when a high volcano, capped with ice, began rumbling in the mountains of Colombia in 1985. On November 13, the ice cap exploded above the town of Armero. The eruption melted snowfields that picked up debris and went roaring down the side of the volcano toward the villages 30 to 40 miles away. The residents were warned that night that a large volcanic mudflow was on the way, Dr. Heiken said. "But it was raining," he said. "People said, 'Why worry, the volcano is far away.' They had only to walk one hundred yards to a hill to be safe. That night, twenty-six thousand people died."

Scientists were horrified, said Dr. Chris Newhall, a volcanologist at the United States Geological Survey at the University of Washington in Seattle. This episode and other natural disasters prompted the United Nations to declare the 1990s the International Decade of Natural Hazard Reduction, he said. "The notion was, look, the world population is growing, the hazards are not getting any less," he said. "People are moving into marginal lands that are more prone to disasters—volcanoes, floods, earthquakes and hurricanes. The basic idea was to encourage countries to take a hard look at the hazards that their populations were facing and to undertake projects to try and reduce risks."

But the United Nations did not have money for the program, Dr. Newhall said. The International Decade of Hazard Reduction has existed in name only.

So the scientists began taking action on their own. Under the auspices of the International Association of Volcanology and Chemistry of the Earth's Interior, "we volcanologists got together and scratched our heads for ideas," Dr. Newhall said. "We came up with three."

First, they made a video that depicts what volcanoes can do to people and property, with such horrifying accuracy that it is not recommended for children under 15. It is being shown to mayors and other public officials in charge of getting people to evacuate when volcanoes threaten to explode.

Second, the scientists picked 15 volcanoes around the world to study intensely. These so-called decade volcanoes are near large population centers and could erupt anytime. Workshops have been held at most of them, bringing together scientists and disaster relief officials from the local regions.

Third, there has been an effort to make better predictions of when volcanoes will erupt, using new scientific instruments and insights.

Although real progress has been made, volcanologists face a couple of intractable problems, Dr. Williams said. One is the tendency for people to deny danger even when it is obvious. Also, once a threat is passed, they tend to dismiss it. "They forget that grandma once told a story about how her grandmother was killed by a volcano," he said. And second is the sheer perversity of volcanoes. They may show all the signs and symptoms of erupting and then quiet down, leading the public to accuse scientists of "crying wolf."

Volcanoes arise from the forces of plate tectonics, and usually occur where great slabs of the Earth's crust are shoved deep into the interior and melted. This molten rock is buoyant, Dr. Williams said, and makes its way back to the surface where it finds a weak spot and explodes to the surface in a volcano.

Most volcanoes live for tens of thousands of years and can remain dormant for centuries between eruptions. The varying amounts of ash, lava and other particles they emit are measured in cubic kilometers, cubes five eighths of a mile on each side. The 1980 Mount St. Helens eruption in Washington State, which devastated the countryside, was a small event by volcanic standards, producing only one cubic kilometer, Dr. Williams said.

By contrast, a volcano in Yellowstone, Wyoming, has over the last two million years spewed out 3,800 cubic kilometers of ash and pumice. If Yellowstone produced another huge eruption, it could shut down the country, he said. Airplanes could not fly, trucks could not deliver food and farmers could not grow crops.

The 15 decade volcanoes are being studied, Dr. Newhall said, "to arrive at a synopsis of what was and was not understood about how each volcano works. Also, what questions need to be addressed to make future forecasts more accurate in terms of the size and timing of eruptions."

First, geologists look all around each volcano, mapping ash deposits and mudflows to determine the nature of each past eruption, how far it went and, with carbon dating, how long ago it happened, said Dr. Richard Fisher, a professor emeritus of geology at the University of California at Santa Barbara. Then they map out hazard zones. If a volcano produced serious damage in one place, it can do so again, he said.

Next, the scientists study the low-frequency earthquakes that these volcanoes tend to produce. Such earthquakes make a special noise that is related to growing magma domes, the ominous bulges formed by molten rock making its way to the surface. With almost every volcano, people in the area begin feeling quakes, hearing noises and smelling gases for days, weeks or months before an eruption, Dr. Williams said. They often sense it is coming.

Using a variety of instruments, the scientists are measuring the size and growth of magma domes at decade volcanoes and the gases they emit. Steam and carbon dioxide indicate that high pressures are building up. Sulfur dioxide emissions "tell you that the magma is in communication with the atmosphere," Dr. Fisher said. It is a definite danger sign.

A few things send volcanologists running for the hills, Dr. Newhall said. If a volcano starts to produce low harmonic tremors, a steady hum of seismic waves, for tens of minutes or hours, it is time to flee. It means magma is rising up the conduit and building gas pressure. Recent studies on decade volcanoes also point to another forewarning: sulfur dioxide levels sometimes drop right before the big blast.

The trouble is, other volcanoes do not give these warning signs before they explode. "You do the best you can," Dr. Newhall said. "You look at spatial and temporal changes and you plot them for weeks, months and then you make your best shot at interpreting what is going on."

The major cause of death in volcanoes is not hot lava or rivers of mud but rather glowing clouds of superhot gas and ash particles that silently sweep down the volcano's flank and across the countryside at 60 miles an hour, vaporizing everything in their path. These pyroclastic flows can knock down stone walls 10 feet thick and have killed thousands of people in less than two minutes, he said. The flows desiccate the flesh and fry the lungs of everyone in their path. Ninety-eight percent of the people in Guatemala live on the surface of a pyroclastic flow that raced over the countryside 75,000 years ago, Dr. Williams said.

From watching volcano movies and films of the rather gentle and atypical volcanoes in Hawaii, people think they can walk away from danger, Dr. Heiken said. The volcanologists' video shows otherwise. It is very blunt and shows dead bodies, he said. "When people see it, they gulp and say, 'Could that really happen here? How far did you say the town was from that volcano?'"

In 1991, a rough cut of the newly made video was rushed to the Philippines, where Mount Pinatubo was threatening to erupt. The day after it was shown on television, 50,000 people evacuated voluntarily. A few days later, the volcano erupted, spewing 12 cubic kilometers of material. "We are convinced that the video saved tens of thousands of lives," Dr. Heiken said.

Getting the word out and convincing people to evacuate is a huge challenge, Dr. Williams said. Ultimately, whether people live or die depends as much on communication as on science. "We try to teach people how not to freak out," he said. "They think falling ash is lethal, but it's not. The problem is that the ash is three times heavier than water so their roof can collapse in hours. We teach people to get under the strongest table in the room, near the corner. The air is full of static electricity, so radios and traffic lights go haywire and they get scared."

Such public education saves lives, Dr. Heiken said. In September 1994, a volcano at Rabaul in Papua New Guinea destroyed 75 percent of the homes in the city. But because the citizens had been trained in evacuation procedures, they did not panic and got away safely. Only five people died.

It is a different story in the United States "where any form of government message is taken as a challenge to people's rights to do whatever they want," Dr. Casadevall said. At Mount St. Helens, some people refused to evacuate and died as a result. Around Mount Rainier, 250,000 people live on the surface of volcanic mudflows that are less than 500 years old. Some older flows reached Seattle. These people are being told they should be ready to move to high ground if Mount Rainier shows signs of erupting, he said. The problem is that with some towns, there is one narrow road out over a single bridge. "We try to make sure people have this information," Dr. Casadevall said, "but if they refuse to leave, they're on their own."

—Sandra Blakeslee, August 1997

Exploring Undersea Birth Throes
of a New Hawaiian Island

RISING FROM DEEP WITHIN THE Earth is a jet of molten rock that cuts gargantuan holes in the Pacific seabed, forming new volcanoes and eventually
whole new islands as well, its brood including Maui and Oahu. Each year,
the jet, the Earth's most intense, spews enough lava to build a road that
would circle the Earth twice. It has been thundering and exploding and
erupting lava for tens of millions of years.

Scientists have descended in a submersible to probe an episode of explosive violence at the jet's leading edge accompanying the birth throes of a
new Hawaiian island. Their target, a half mile down, was the summit of
Loihi, which has suddenly become one of the world's most active volcanoes.

"It's nerve-racking," Dr. Alexander Malahoff, the expedition's chief scientist, said of his dives into the dark, churning waters. "The top of the volcano is a physical wreck."

In July and August of 1996, the site was rocked by thousands of
seaquakes, including the strongest ever recorded around Hawaii. Since the
volcanic seamount is only 17 miles southeast of the big island of Hawaii,
disaster officials feared that the deep violence might set off tidal waves at
the surface that could devastate the big island as well as more distant
shores of Oahu, including Honolulu and Waikiki Beach.

Land was in fact spared. But Dr. Malahoff and the other scientists who
dove to the craggy recesses of the undersea volcano discovered a riot of
landslides, toppled rock formations and bus-size volcanic boulders strewn
over four or five miles. But this was not the result of a major eruption. The
turmoil at the volcano's top had collapsed its summit, creating a murky
crater more than a half-mile wide and 1,000 feet deep.

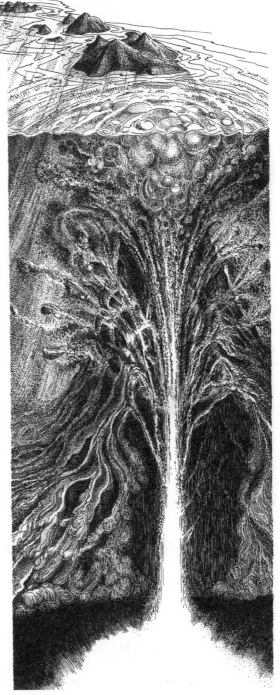

"Emerging Link in a Chain"
As the Pacific plate moves over a volcanic hot spot, islands rise and sink. The latest, Loihi, is almost three miles high and within half a mile of the surface.

The march of the Pacific plate is traced in a long line of islands, with a dogleg to the east where the plate changed directions about 40 million years ago. The volcanic forces forming Loihi have now been directly observed, after thousands of recent earthquakes and a major collapse of the seamount's peak, which left a crater half a mile wide and a thousand feet deep. (*The New York Times;* Illustration by Dimitry Schidlovsky)

Intense seismic activity in and around the Loihi seamount summit has recently resulted in a major collapse of part of the bulge, an area now called Pele's Pit. Some of the other major pits and ridges show clearly in this reconstruction made from data obtained by instruments aboard a submersible vessel. The field shown here is about 6 miles wide by 13 miles long.
(Source: Dr. Alexander Malaholff/University of Hawaii at Manoa; J.R. Smith (original map))

"This was a Mount St. Helens–size volcanic event," Dr. Malahoff said. "Pete's Dome, an area on the southern rim of the volcano that previously had been considered very stable, has simply vanished."

He made three dives into the volcanic depths in as many days in late September of 1996, and the dives will continue. The team is diving in a Pisces submersible, which can carry three people down a little more than a mile and is therefore limited to exploring the volcano's summit. The whole seamount rises almost three miles from the ocean floor. Dr. Malahoff is director of the Hawaii Undersea Research Laboratory at the University of Hawaii, and the dives are financed by the National Oceanic and Atmospheric Administration.

Diving into the new crater, Dr. Malahoff found vents spewing a mixture of superheated water, dissolved minerals and microbes that thrive in the seabed's rocky substratum. Churning clouds of particles often limited visibility to about a yard or less.

And tricky currents posed dangers. Waters flowed into the newly formed pit, percolated through the volcano's hot interior and rushed out over a lip on the volcano's western edge. The scientists had to avoid getting sucked down by the inrush on one side and pushed up by the outrush on the other.

They say the tumult is part of the volcano's halting upward growth. Lava flows build it up, and avalanches and collapses and cataclysmic explosions knock it down and widen it, creating a larger base for the next stage of building. Tens of thousands of years are expected to pass before the volcano's fiery summit rises above the waves.

"The fight is between construction and destruction," Dr. Malahoff said.

Avalanches are well known to have shaken the steep sides of Loihi, but no episode this violent has ever before been studied up close. Scientists say the event sheds important new light on the dynamics of island building as well as a whole range of environmental issues, like the extent to which explosive releases of volcanic gases like carbon dioxide may be contributing to the greenhouse warming of the Earth. Such releases, they say, may augment human-caused releases.

And it is aiding overall studies of the Hawaiian jet, the Earth's most dynamic zone of volcanic upheaval. Beneath the big island of Hawaii it powers the fireworks of both the Kilauea and Mauna Loa volcanoes.

"We think it is rather large, as much as two hundred kilometers in diameter," or about 125 miles, Dr. James G. Moore, a geologist with the United States Geological Survey in Menlo Park, California, said in an interview. "Loihi is the first manifestation of volcanic activity on that crust," added Dr. Moore, who has studied the Hawaiian volcanoes. "It's the leading edge."

The great heat engine within the Earth stirs a sea of hot plastic rock that melts through the crust in places, with the vast majority of the surface action taking place in the hidden darkness of the deep sea.

In places, the interior heat gives birth to jets, or plumes of hot material, that are stationary in relation to the deep Earth but continuously rise toward the surface. Over the eons, the jets pierce crustal plates that move slowly overhead, much as a fixed blowtorch would melt holes in a steel plate moving by.

The gigantic plates that make up the Earth's crust move over the jets at the rate of a few centimeters a year, or about as fast as fingernails grow.

As a result of this slow creep, a single jet over the ages can leave a trail of extinct, progressively older volcanoes in the plate above. Such a trail is seen in the Pacific, where the Hawaiian hot spot has formed not only the Loihi volcano but a chain of extinct ones that run westward across the Pacific plate from Hawaii and then turns northward to form the Emperor seamount chain, extending to the northwest corner of the ocean. In all, the chain covers thousands of miles and mirrors tens of millions of years of volcanic action.

The bend where the Hawaiian chain turns into the Emperor chain represents a change of plate motion that occurred about 40 million years ago.

The volcanic islands are slowly pared down by landslides and sink deeper into the sea, usually leaving only the newer ones at the head of the chain above water—or struggling to break through the waves.

Loihi, which means "long one" in Hawaiian and is pronounced low-EE-hee, is an elongated monster eight miles wide and 15.5 miles long. The Pacific seabed on which it rests is 3.4 miles down at its lowest point. During eruptions and outbursts over tens of thousands of years, Loihi has grown until the volcano is now more than 2.8 miles tall.

Its stirrings are carefully monitored by several government agencies, including the National Oceanic and Atmospheric Administration, an arm of the Commerce Department, and the United States Geological Survey, which maintains a network of seismometers on the big island. Seismometers measure faint vibrations in the ground that tell of distant earthquakes.

Loihi has heaved with seaquakes before, most recently in 1991, but not like this recent torrent of violence. The quakes prompted Harry Kim, the Civil Defense director of Hawaii County, which encompasses the big island, to warn residents to head for higher ground immediately if they felt an earthquake, since there would be no time for sirens or emergency broadcasts before a tidal wave struck.

Island residents are used to coping with threats of tidal waves generated by distant earthquakes far across the ocean but not local ones.

To better understand what was happening and, in part, to help develop ways to predict and warn of future dangers, Dr. Malahoff and his team dove into the depths.

"Eventually something will happen," he said of disasters on land touched off by the deep volcano, "but maybe not in our lifetimes."

In trying to unravel the mystery of the deep upheaval, the team early on monitored the violence with microphones suspended from buoys and detected cracklings that sounded like the flow of deep lava. But submersible probings of the volcano's northern summit in the area of the cracklings revealed no new flows, only old ones.

What the team did discover, based on a comparison with older observations, was that a huge part of the volcano's summit had collapsed in the frenzy of destruction. "Nobody," Dr. Malahoff said, "has ever observed the formation of these pit craters."

The collapse of the summit probably took two or three days, he said, and its slowness was a godsend. A quick collapse would have generated a huge tsunami, or tidal wave. He said the gaping pit was big enough to hold the contents of 50 million dump trucks.

A likely possibility, he said, is that the slow collapse was provoked when hot lava from the volcano's interior oozed out of its flanks at a depth somewhere below the region where the Pisces submersible could explore.

"Fifty million dump trucks of lava has gone somewhere," he mused, adding that the issue remained a major mystery.

In the most dangerous moment of the series of dives, Dr. Malahoff and two colleagues ventured down to the bottom of the new crater past fractured walls of towering rocks that were threatening to fall. Later, at the crater's bottom 1,000 feet below the summit, the anxious team in the submersible heard the rumble of a distant landslide.

At the base of the huge cliff, the team found a big vent belching hot water and clouds of microbial snow, the area around the vent painted with orange and red bacterial mats and flapping lettucelike leaves of bacterial slime.

"It's eerie," Dr. Malahoff said at the news conference as he showed a videotape of the crater floor taken by the submersible's cameras. "It looks like a haunted house."

The team, he said, was surprised how quickly life had taken root in an area shaken weeks earlier by cataclysmic violence. "Here they are swarming," he said, pointing to a microbial mass.

Fifty thousand years might pass before the young volcano grows high enough to pierce the surface, Dr. Malahoff said. And in the meantime, Loihi had much to teach scientists about the way the Earth works in its most secretive regions, building and breaking, creating and destroying.

The deep region, he predicted, will be torn by "all kinds of throes" that the scientists want to study.

—WILLIAM J. BROAD, October 1996

Ice Sheets Seem Unmoved by the Volcanic Eruptions Below

WHEN VOLCANOES ERUPT BENEATH THICK sheets of ice, the resulting flash floods sometimes devastate communities, roads and farms. But there is new evidence that the effects of these eruptions are mostly local, with little overall effect on the ice sheets themselves.

Scientists have a special reason for worrying about subglacial volcanoes. Since 1993, it has been known that volcanoes have been erupting under the ice sheet covering West Antarctica. If geothermal heat associated with volcanic activity should create a wide layer of water beneath this ice, it has been speculated, the water might moisten the volcanic ash on which much of the ice rests, creating a lubricant on which the ice might slide. If the West Antarctic Ice Sheet were to slide into the ocean, the sea level would rise by 65 feet worldwide, flooding low-lying nations like Bangladesh and the Netherlands and causing a global catastrophe.

A new study of volcanic activity beneath Iceland's Vatnajokull ice cap suggests that some subglacial eruptions have little long-term effect on the stability of ice sheets. This reassuring conclusion was reported in the October 30, 1997, issue of the journal *Nature* by Dr. Helgi Bjornsson and his colleagues at the University of Iceland in Reykjavik.

The object of their investigation was a 13-day eruption that occurred when a subglacial volcano blasted its way through a fissure named Gjalp (after a mythological giantess) and up through ice nearly a half-mile thick. The eruption sent plumes of steam and ash some 33,000 feet into the air and melted one-half cubic mile of ice.

For five weeks, water melted by the eruption flowed into a subglacial lake, which finally overflowed, unleashing a flood that destroyed bridges, cut roads and felled power lines. But because Icelandic experts had given ample warning of the flood, the region had been evacuated and there were no casualties.

Such floods occur every five to 10 years, Dr. Bjornsson said in an interview, because the ice cap covers a geological hot spot that continuously melts ice. The periodic overflow of the subglacial lake, he said, has created a channel some 30 miles long under the ice, leading to the edge of the glacier. The subglacial channel serves as a duct for the flood water.

Dr. Bjornsson and his colleagues concluded on the basis of aerial surveys and ground measurements that the ice cap was not significantly changed by the 1996 eruption and that it remains firmly anchored to underlying bedrock.

On October 13, 1996, when the eruption ended, the peak of a new volcanic mountain appeared above the surface of an ice cauldron formed by the eruption. "But we know that the mountain peak will disappear in a few years because new ice is already filling in the cauldron," Dr. Bjornsson said.

Dr. Donald D. Blankenship of the University of Texas at Austin, a leading expert on the West Antarctic Ice Sheet, said observations made of the Icelandic eruption did not necessarily apply to Antarctica.

"There are big differences between Iceland and Antarctica," he said. "For one thing, the ice sheet in Antarctica is up to nine thousand feet thick, while its Icelandic counterpart is only twenty-five hundred feet thick."

Dr. Blankenship said that relatively little was known about the geology underlying the West Antarctic Ice Sheet but that a system of Antarctic channels, similar to those in Iceland, might exist—channels that could carry meltwater away from regions of volcanic activity. If so, he said, there could be local volcanic effects on the ice sheet but no general melting at its base, and therefore no major sliding.

"There's a growing consensus among glaciologists that subglacial volcanoes in West Antarctica are unlikely to have a major impact on the stability of the ice sheet," he said.

—MALCOLM W. BROWNE, December 1997

El Popo's Rumblings Draw
Volcanologists to Edge of Danger

IN 1993, six volcanologists studying the Galeras volcano, a smoky colossus in the Colombian Andes, died when it exploded in a riot of lava, ash and incandescent boulders, some flung miles high. Dr. Stanley N. Williams, a seventh member of the team gathering data in the crater at the time of the eruption, lived to tell about it, though with a fractured skull, crushed ear, broken nose, broken jaw, broken legs and extensive burns.

Now healed and armed with a new instrument, he is headed for Popocatepetl, a 3.4-mile-high volcano 45 miles from Mexico City whose peak is covered year round by snow. El Popo, as it is called, shows signs of getting ready to explode, threatening one of the most populous regions on Earth, as well as important ruins, like Cholula, site of the 40-acre, 230-foot Tepanapa Pyramid, one of the largest in the Americas.

Despite his close call, Dr. Williams is anything but ready to give up volcanology.

"I'm going to work on Popo because it's an exciting opportunity to test this instrument—and because it demands attention," Dr. Williams said in an interview, pointing out that it was a huge volcano next to one of the biggest cities in the world.

But as he renews his acquaintance with slumbering giants, Dr. Williams plans to stay far from the volcano's rocky crater, which has repeatedly exploded in a frenzy of blistering lava and ash over the centuries. In a way, he has learned his lesson.

His new instrument works by reading volcanic gases from a distance, using a small telescope linked to a chemical sensor. During field trials, he hopes to analyze gases from the volcanic plume and detect symptoms of an impending explosion—all from a relatively safe range of up to 20 or 25

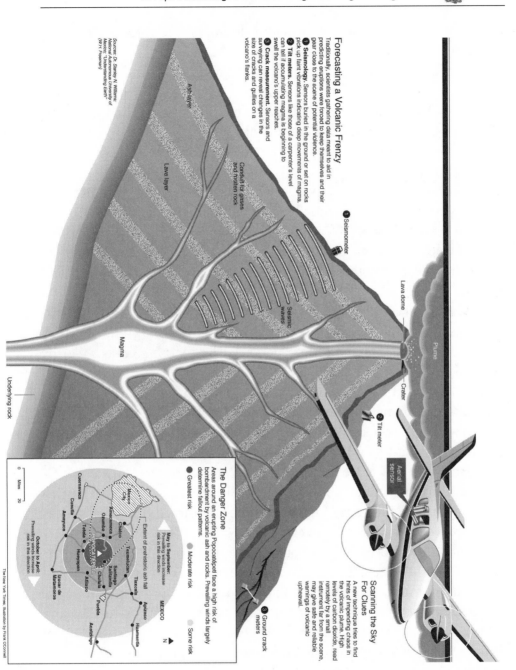

Forecasting a Volcanic Frenzy

Traditionally, scientists gathering data meant to aid in predicting eruptions were forced to keep themselves and their gear close to the scene of potential violence.

① Seismology. Sensors buried in the ground or set on rocks pick up faint vibrations indicating deep movements of magma.

② Tilt meters. Sensors like those of a carpenter's level can tell if accumulating magma is beginning to swell the volcano's upper reaches.

③ Crack measurement. Sensors and surveying can reveal changes in the size of cracks and gullies on a volcano's flanks.

Ash layer

Lava layer

Magma

Underlying rock

Conduit for gases and molten rock

Seismic waves

① Seismometer

Lava dome

Crater

Plume

② Tilt meter

Aerial sensor

③ Ground crack meters

Scanning the Sky For Clues

A new technique tries to find hints of impending chaos in the volcanic plume. High levels of carbon dioxide, read remotely by a small instrument far from the scene, may give safe and reliable warnings of volcanic upheaval.

The Danger Zone

Areas around an erupting Popocatépetl face a high risk of bombardment by volcanic ash and rocks. Prevailing winds largely determine fallout patterns.

● Greatest risk

● Moderate risk

● Some risk

Extent of prehistoric ash fall

May to September: Prevailing winds increase risk in this direction

October to April: Prevailing winds increase risk in this direction

POPOCATÉPETL

MEXICO

N

Mexico City
Cuernavaca
Cuautla
Amayuca
Tetela
Huejotzingo
Amecameca
Chalco
Ozumba
Texmelucan
Santiago Xalitzintla
Atlixco
Cholula
Tlaxcala
Apizaco
Huamantla
Izúcar de Matamoros
Acatzingo
Puebla

Miles
0   20

Sources: Dr. Stanley N. Williams, National Autonomous University of Mexico; "Understanding Earth" (W.H. Freeman)

The New York Times; Illustration by Frank O'Connell

miles. He can do the research as he travels around the volcano's base in a rental car.

Even so, Dr. Williams cannot resist the temptation to get a bit closer to his quarry in a bid to compare the ground readings with those taken higher up. And so he also plans to fly his instrument aboard a friend's airplane, passing beneath the volcano's smoky plume.

Peers of Dr. Williams applaud his dedication and say his approach has great technical merit. They also commend the work because it promises to save lives—not only those of people who live near volcanoes but of volcanologists because it can potentially work far from the areas of greatest risk.

"Gas measurements offer a tremendous amount of promise," said Bill Rose, a volcanologist at Michigan Technological University in Houghton, who works on such instrumentation. "Stan is trying to make them safe and reliable."

With a hint of defensiveness, Dr. Rose added, of himself and all volcanologists, "None of us in this business are trying to get blown up."

Popocatepetl (pronounced po-po-ka-TEH-pe-tal) is seen as a worthy object of study not only because of its current menace but because it has repeatedly proved its deadliness by devastating human settlements over the ages. In studying earthen samples and cores from its flanks, geologists have discovered that the giant has gone through three major cycles of eruption in the last 5,000 years, most recently from A.D. 675 to 1095.

Such eruptions made the central Mexican plateau not only a dangerous place for early settlers but, paradoxically, attractive as well. The rich volcanic soil was a bonanza for agriculture and fostered the rise of the region's sprawling pre-Colombian cultures.

During the most recent eruption cycle, the smoking mountain (the meaning of Popocatepetl in the local language) spewed enough ash and lava and mud from melted snow and ice to all but bury a nearby town. Claus Siebe of the National Autonomous University in Mexico City, and three colleagues, writing *Geology,* a journal of the Geological Society of America, suggest that the eruption destroyed the great ceremonial center at nearby Cholula, "essentially leaving the pyramids sticking out of a muddy wasteland."

The decline from A.D. 800 to 900 of Cholula, probably the oldest continuously occupied town in Mexico, has long been an archeological riddle.

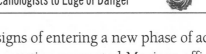

Of late Popocatepetl has shown signs of entering a new phase of activity. On December 21, 1994, a minor eruption prompted Mexican officials to evacuate 75,000 people from its eastern flank, the site believed to be most vulnerable to disaster. Ever since, officials and geologists have labored to monitor its pulse more effectively, hoping to avoid mayhem.

Among the monitoring techniques used routinely around the world, one of the best and least intrusive is to track the movements of hot magma beneath the volcano with sensitive arrays of seismographs that detect Earth tremors. Once sensors are buried, they can be left alone while their signals are sent to a remote spot where scientists try to track the upward migration of magma, the term for molten rock before its release at the surface as hot lava.

Such techniques can reveal trends but often fail to pin down specifics. For that, closer monitoring is often required. For instance, much can be disclosed by measuring cracks and swellings on a volcano's dome and flanks as well as by measure of changes in the composition of vented gases to track the arrival of fresh magma—and to warn of fast-rising danger.

Recently Popocatepetl has been releasing about 10,000 tons of sulfur dioxide daily, scientists calculate, indicating that a huge reservoir of relatively old magma sits deep beneath its craggy rim. The question of interest to Dr. Williams and many other scientists is whether that enormous flow of hot gas is being joined by increasing amounts of carbon dioxide, indicating an influx of newer, more dangerous magma.

The tracking of carbon dioxide from slumbering volcanoes usually requires that the sensors be placed in the plume itself by volcanologists who hike into the zone of extreme danger. What Dr. Williams is trying to do, with financing from the National Science Foundation, a federal agency that sponsors basic research, is to develop the means to make such measurements remotely.

"The big advantage is that I don't have to get blown up again," Dr. Williams said. "I can drive or fly. It doesn't have to be close."

The new instrument is basically a white box about a foot by a foot by 18 inches. Highly computerized, it collects light from the smoky plumes with its telescope and analyzes it for the presence of the carbon dioxide, which is revealed by a slight glow in the infrared part of the electromagnetic spectrum. Because the device responds to emitted light rather than sunlight reflected off the plume, it can work day and night.

"It looks a little bit warm against the sky," Robert Dick, an official at Barringer Research, a company in suburban Toronto that is helping Dr. Williams design the instrument, said of the carbon-dioxide glow.

So far, the instrument has been tested against plumes from electric power plants in Canada and the United States, which release carbon dioxide from burning fuels. The planned test in Mexico will be the first volcanic surveillance.

The plan is to drive and fly beneath Popocatepetl's smoky plume, comparing the readings underneath with those of the nearby sky.

One challenge is to distinguish the carbon dioxide in the atmosphere from that added by the volcano. Carbon dioxide in air naturally occurs at a level of about 350 parts per million. Popocatepetl might add enough carbon dioxide so that the plume, after the dispersion and dilution that occurs as it drifts away, might give readings no more than one to 10 parts per million above that background level. An additional challenge is the haze of the central Mexican plateau, which is rich in carbon dioxide added from cars and factories.

But if Dr. Williams can track the volcanic changes at a safe distance, he is confident that he can help save lives, perhaps thousands of them.

"It's a new instrument," Dr. Williams said, allowing that unforeseen trouble might hamper its performance. But if everything works right, he said, he is confident that he can get about six miles downwind, and possibly 25 to 30 miles from the volcano to look for signs of trouble.

"We know that the ratio of carbon dioxide to sulfur dioxide is going to be changing," he said. "We want to know the envelope of nature's noise," of the natural variation in the volcano's gases. And ultimately, Dr. Williams added, "we want to know when Popo is going out of that envelope and is ready to blow."

—WILLIAM J. BROAD, May 1996

U.S. Scientists Get Rare Glimpse of a Russian Volcano "Lab"

WHEN THE SHIVELUCH VOLCANO ERUPTED in 1964 it took Yuri Dubik, a Russian volcanologist, 10 days by dog sled to reach the smoldering peak near an ultrasecret Soviet military base on the Kamchatka Peninsula, Russia's eastern frontier.

After collecting ash, temperature readings and other data, which would later contribute to scientists' understanding of deadly blasts like the one in 1980 at Mount St. Helens in Washington State, Mr. Dubik returned to his laboratory at the Institute of Volcanology here. A pile of telegrams from the United States was waiting.

"The Americans suddenly had taken a strong interest in Shiveluch," recalled Mr. Dubik, 56, a veteran of 21 volcanic eruptions. "The telegrams contained all sorts of strange questions. Maybe they were trying to learn something about the base. Maybe they thought an atomic bomb exploded. We did our best to assure them Shiveluch really did erupt."

Nearly 30 years later American scientists have studied the volcanoes of Kamchatka up close in the first joint mission with Russian scientists here in one of the richest natural volcanic laboratories in the world. Squeezed into an area the size of Montana, Kamchatka's 160 volcanoes, 29 of them active, offer examples of the entire range of volcanic activity seen on Earth over the last 50 million years.

The monthlong research expedition, completed in September of 1993, should help scientists better understand volcanic eruptions, their frequency and magnitude, and their effect on the atmosphere, the National Aeronautics and Space Administration, which participated in the work, said in Washington.

Western volcanologists heard very little about the work being done by their Russian colleagues until 1991, when restrictions on visiting there were lifted. Even most Russians needed special permission to visit.

The possible effects of eruptions from the volcanoes are causing new alarm. The American scientists said volcanic ash from Shiveluch, Bezimyannyi, Klyuchevskoi and other volcanoes could damage the protective ozone layer in the atmosphere and interfere with air traffic in the busy international air corridor windward of the 800-mile-long peninsula.

One of the most active volcanoes, Shiveluch appeared 50,000 to 60,000 years ago at the intersection of two volcanic fronts—one running north to south through Kamchatka, the other east to west through Alaska and the Aleutian Islands. After Shiveluch last erupted in April 1992, a potentially explosive dome grew in its crater.

Built from alternating layers of ash and lava by eruptions over 5,000 years, Klyuchevskoi is one of the biggest volcanoes in the world. It measures 15,500 feet, its icy rim towering above the clouds. More than 100 small cones, called parasite volcanoes, cover its slopes like warts.

The research was carried out by the Joint Implementation Team for Volcanology, under an agreement between the Russian Academy of Sciences and NASA. Using remote sensing, the seven-member Russian team and the 16-member American team, which included a Russian copilot, began mapping the area and monitored volcanic emissions. The group was trying to evaluate the danger volcanic ash poses to the ozone layer and air traffic. The United States scientists were also hoping to learn more about what makes a volcano erupt.

"Kamchatka is the missing link in our understanding of the Ring of Fire," said Dr. David C. Pieri, the leader of the team, referring to the active volcanoes that circle the Pacific basin, wedding beauty and destruction. More than 500 of these volcanoes, including Mount Fuji in Japan, Krakatoa in Indonesia, Pinatubo in the Philippines, Mount St. Helens in Washington, Mount Redoubt in Alaska and the Hawaiian Islands, form the violent perimeter. The Kamchatka volcanoes make up an 800-mile sector of the Ring of Fire.

According to the Institute of Volcanology, Kamchatka's hyperactive volcanoes pump out 16 to 17 percent of all the ash, lava and rock produced by the Earth's 850 active volcanoes. While volcanoes near the Equator erupt

far below the ozone layer, those in polar regions like Kamchatka ṛ
more of a threat, especially during the winter, when the strato-spṛ
taining the ozone layer drops to about 15,000 feet. "Any matter tṛ
into that layer stays there," said Dr. Pieri, a volcanologist at the Jet Pṛ
sion Laboratory at the California Institute of Technology in Pasadena.

Noting "an arguable link" between volcanic eruptions and ozone loss,
Dr. Pieri warned, "The Russian volcanoes have a good chance of damaging
the ozone layer."

Large amounts of volcanic ash can also endanger airplane crews and
passengers. After emissions from Mount Redoubt caused all four engines
of a Boeing 747 to flame out in 1989 over Alaska, airline pilots and NASA
began to worry about Kamchatka. "It's a shooting gallery of volcanoes
across here," said Dr. Pieri.

Easterly winds carry the ash into air lanes used by more than 10,000
people a day flying between North America and Southeast Asia. Dr. Pieri
said the NASA team was unraveling the spectral properties of Kamchatka's
volcanic sulfur dioxide emissions.

That information could be used to set up satellite monitoring of the
northern Pacific rim to steer pilots away from ash clouds. Weather satellites are already used to detect eruptions in Japan, the United States, Mexico and Central America, but that information sometimes takes 12 hours to
reach air traffic controllers.

Dr. Pieri said a follow-up mission is not on the horizon. It took five
years to persuade the Russians to allow NASA to fly a Learjet equipped
with a $1.2 million thermal infrared multispectral scanner over one of
Russia's most sensitive areas. The instrument collected data that can be
used to make maps of surface temperatures and to analyze the chemical
compounds in lava.

Having only recently begun to study the environmental impact of volcanoes, the Russian volcanologists have been deciphering eruptions to find
out what is happening under the Earth's crust and to piece together a history of the Earth.

Except for the Avanchansky volcano, which unexpectedly erupted
in 1991, covering Petropavlosk-Kamchatsky in ash, and Klyuchevskoi,
whose lava flows threaten a nearby town of 15,000, Kamchatka's volcanoes
erupt deep in the wilderness and have claimed few lives.

Mr. Dubik counted them on his fingers. "Five, six—all volcanologists and mostly on the slopes of Klyuchevskoi," he said.

Choosing Kamchatka in 1961 over graduate studies at Moscow State University, Mr. Dubik has spent more than one night on the craters of erupting volcanoes "to get a better look inside," as he put it.

Lacking high technology, Russian volcanologists have resorted to what Dr. Pieri called "brute force" to explore Kamchatka. "They go out there and climb the damn volcano, " he said.

"The Russians have done a beautiful job dating ash and an extremely delicate job categorizing and timing eruptions. We can use that information to expand our knowledge of all eruptions."

As for the Russian volcanologists, they are suffering from budget cuts and infighting. Last year the Institute of Volcanology split into two opposing camps sharing one building.

Forced to sit out two recent eruptions because the institute could not afford to finance expeditions, Mr. Dubik hesitated to predict which volcano on Kamchatka may be next. "The biggies here have all had their say for the next fifty to one hundred years," he replied. "It's the others we're worried about. The ones that haven't exploded yet in the history of man."

—SUZANNE POSSEHL, November 1993

The Gradual Greening of Mount St. Helens

WHEN THE MOUNT ST. HELENS volcano exploded in 1980, the north slope collapsed with a mighty shudder and sent an avalanche of mud and rock down into the valley of the Toutle River. Every tree in sight—nearly every sprig of vegetation within 15 miles of the erupting crater—was swept away or buried, leaving a virtually lifeless terrain.

Life is hardy, though, and each year the gray swath of avalanche debris becomes a shade greener. Biologists and ecologists who study the revegetation of the stricken land are encouraged by the gradual comeback, although they are chagrined to discover yet another case in which nature would probably have been better off if people had left well enough alone.

From buried seeds, pieces of root and dormant growth buds, vegetation native to the slopes is slowly returning—trees like willow, red alder and hemlock seedlings and plants like fireweed, thistle and lupine. A new study shows that 83 plant species, of a total of 256 known to have been there before the eruption, have been identified in the area of the avalanche. Almost 20 percent of the surface is now covered with grass, legumes and struggling young trees.

But alien plants introduced in an effort to reduce erosion in the immediate aftermath seem to be inhibiting recovery of the native species, according to findings by Dr. Virginia H. Dale, a mathematician and ecologist at the Oak Ridge National Laboratory in Tennessee. She was one of the first scientists to inspect the volcanic devastation in 1980 and has made periodic surveys of plant recovery at 97 plots in the avalanche area.

Dr. Dale determined that on plots where exotic plants made up more than 10 percent of the vegetation cover, the native plants and especially

39

coniferous trees were struggling to gain a foothold. Conifers, such as hemlock and Douglas fir, were the dominant trees in the preeruption forests. But their survival and growth were threatened by competition from introduced species, such as the robust cloverlike plant *Lotus corniculatus*, a legume commonly known as birdsfoot trefoil.

"*Lotus* is reducing the abundance of native species rather than enhancing the recovery process," Dr. Dale concluded in a report published in *Research & Exploration*, a journal of the National Geographic Society. The society helped finance the research, and volunteers from Earthwatch, an ecological research organization in Watertown, Massachusetts, assisted in the fieldwork two years ago.

Dr. Dale suggested that the alien grasses deprived the native species of moisture and scarce nutrients. Also, she said, the abundance of seeds from the dense alien grass caused the mouse population to rise sharply. The mice then killed many young conifers by chewing bark off the trees in the winter, accounting for as much as 55 percent of conifer mortality before predators, hawks and coyotes, became more numerous and began reducing the mouse population.

"By studying the process of natural revegetation of such denuded sites and the consequences of human intereference, scientists will be able to improve prescriptions for reclamation of other areas," Dr. Dale said in the report.

She said in a telephone interview that the exact mechanism by which the alien species stymied recovery of native species was not known. At best, she added, "it will definitely be more than a hundred years," before life on the mountain's slopes is likely to return to some kind of normality.

Dr. Donald Zobel, a botanist at Oregon State University, said, "Patches of green are showing up, especially on steep hills where debris has eroded away. But there's still a lot of gray surface where there were forests that got blasted away."

Other scientists are conducting similar studies of the revegetation of other types of devastated terrain at the volcano. The areas of investigation include the crater itself, where no life survived and little has been reintroduced; the pyroclastic zone, where the explosive rain of hot gases probably left no survivors and the surface remains virtually barren; the blowdown zone, where all trees were toppled by the wind from the volcanic blast, but ground plants survived; and the scorch zone, at the perimeter where heat singed tree leaves but did not leave much permanent damage.

In the avalanche area where Dr. Dale has concentrated observations, deposits of mud and rock extend 15 miles down from the crater and are more than a mile wide and an average of 140 feet deep.

Scientists familiar with research on the volcano's revegetation said Dr. Dale's study points out the continuing increase in the variety of species on the slopes and the apparent adverse effect of introduced species on native plant recovery.

The consequences might have been worse.

Immediately after the eruption, government officials and scientists were concerned about the potential effects of erosion and further landslides in the devastated areas, particularly where the avalanche had occurred. The Soil Conservation Service of the Department of Agriculture proposed to distribute seeds of grasses and legumes over most of the area to prevent erosion. When other scientists objected to the introduction of exotic species, the seeding was restricted to an outlying area.

The seeds were the standard varieties used along roadsides for erosion control. Besides the birdsfoot trefoil, there were ryegrass, orchardgrass and tall fescue. Within a year, half of the seeded area was covered in the exotic species, which were spreading. Blown by wind and carried by animals, the seeds found their way into the primary avalanche debris deposits, and in several places began crowding out native species.

Moreover, Dr. Dale noted, in the areas originally seeded, the introduced species "were ineffective in mitigating the major erosion problem— large-scale channel erosion into streams."

Recognizing the mistake, the Soil Conservation Service's 26 research stations around the country have begun collecting natural species and having their seeds available for future erosion-control operations, said Jack Carlson, an official of the agency in Portland, Oregon.

Dr. Dale said nurseries specializing in commercial quantities of native species are becoming more common and "should be considered in revegetation planning."

Species that have their growth hormones stored in buds or bulbs that occur below the surface tended to be among the first plants to flourish after the eruption. The most conspicuous have been the willows, some reaching heights of 12 feet, and some hardy stands of young cottonwood and red alder.

Scientists are watching the trees with particular interest; if the lower slopes of Mount St. Helens ever return to normal, they should be thickly forested with fir, hemlock, cottonwood, alder and, along streams, several varieties of willow.

—JOHN NOBLE WILFORD, October 1991

2

EARTHQUAKES

Lithosphere

Oceanic trench

Serpentine

Olivine

Spinel

Perovskite and oxide

63 MILES

249 MILES

418 MILES

Area of detail

● Deep-focus quakes

Earthquakes are periodic reminders that some of the bedrock facts people take for granted are unfounded. Terra firma can be suddenly become terra jello. Solid buildings shake and shiver. Bridges fall, highways shear. Some 50,000 earthquakes occur every year, most of them too small to notice. But a hundred or so are large enough to cause damage. And every few decades a city is obliterated with horrifying loss of life.

On November 1, 1755, an earthquake shattered Lisbon, the capital of Portugal. Since it was All Saints' Day, many people were in church, an unfortunate place to be since all the churches in the city were destroyed. A fire then started that raged for six days. By the time it was over, 60,000 people had died.

The earthquake that struck San Francisco in 1906 killed only 700 people, but the ensuing fires razed the city's business district. Far more destructive was the 1923 earthquake that leveled much of the Tokyo-Yokohama district in Japan, killing 140,000 people.

An enormous earthquake hit Alaska in 1964 but killed few people because most of the affected areas were sparsely inhabited. The next quake was less merciful: in 1976, 240,000 people were killed, and some 500,000 injured, in the Chinese city of T'ang-shan. The earthquake struck at night, and many people were crushed in their beds as their houses collapsed on top of them.

The most recent large earthquake hit Mexico in 1985 with a toll of 10,000 people dead.

Despite long-standing hopes that earthquakes could be predicted, geophysicists have so far failed to find any method of forecasting their time of occurrence. But better understanding of their mechanism enables the likely places to be defined. Earthquakes are generated at the boundaries between the several large tectonic plates of which the Earth's crust is composed. Unfortunately many of these earthquake-prone zones include coastal areas where large cities are located, such as San Francisco, Los Angeles and Tokyo.

Building codes, if they have been scrupulously followed, should reduce the loss of life in these cities when the next earthquake strikes. Still, these terrifying phenomena remain untamable and unpredictable.

Seismologists Debate
Los Angeles's Faults

BURIED DEEP BENEATH THE FREEWAYS, shopping malls and luxurious homes of Los Angeles there lies a network of faults that could literally turn parts of this city upside down.

The faults are oriented in such a way that should they suddenly snap and produce a large earthquake, energy would be focused upward, moving like rockets fired from millions of submerged submarines. Objects and people directly overhead would be lifted into the air, momentarily weightless, as the earthquake waves shuddered past.

The faults are called blind thrusts. They are "blind" because they do not break through to the surface, and scientists cannot see them directly. They are thrusts because when they break, one side of the fault moves up over the other at a steep angle, focusing energy toward the surface. Mountains, hills, folds and scarps are formed in the process.

Thrust faults tend to focus energy directly toward the surface, said Dr. David Schwartz, a researcher at the United States Geological Survey in Menlo Park, California. If enough energy is released, people and objects overcome the Earth's gravitational field and rise into the air. During the 1971 Sylmar earthquake in the San Fernando Valley, earthquake researchers say, a fire truck lifted off the ground inside the firehouse before plopping back down.

On the other hand, the faults may slip gradually so that energy is released upward ever so slowly, giving gentle birth to hills like those that dot the Los Angeles basin. Malibu, Beverly Hills and the Hollywood Hills are all products of blind-thrust faults.

Geologists call it the "Los Angeles earthquake dilemma" and among geophysical problems, it is a big one. Experts agree that there are major faults under the city, but they do not know how dangerous they are, when they last broke and how big an earthquake, if any, they could produce.

So each day for the last couple of years, local scientists have fanned out over the basin in search of answers. They are measuring infinitesimal ground motions, peering into excavations freshly cut for storm sewers and underground parking lots, and examining oil seeps in Malibu and Beverly Hills. They are also "thumping" surface streets to obtain sonographic images of the Earth's crust. Thumpers are essentially flat-bottomed jackhammers that send sound waves three to six miles down. Listening devices called geophones pick up the reflected sound waves, whose patterns reveal geologic structures.

Plans are afoot to run thumpers down several residential streets in Santa Monica and, if permission can be obtained, to close some freeway sections in the wee hours of the morning and run thumpers down them.

An even larger experiment involves firing an air gun off the coast and capturing reflected waves from the Earth's crust. The researchers hope to get a good view of structures under the mountains north of Los Angeles.

"These blind-thrust faults under L.A. are five miles down," Dr. Schwartz said. "You really can't put your hands on them. Just defining where they are and their extent relies on modeling and a lot of interpretation.

"We are in a funny position of saying to people, 'Look, we have this hazard here but we don't know the size of it, we don't know how often it moves and we don't know its geometry. It's a scary structure, if it exists. Yes, it would be bad if it moves, but we can't give you a probability. It could happen tomorrow or in a thousand years.' It's not a very satisfying answer, but that's where we are."

With this uncertainty in mind, the Southern California Earthquake Consortium was established two and a half years ago with funds from the National Science Foundation. Scientists from a dozen institutions are trying to assess the buried faults and advise local disaster-preparedness officials about the dangers.

Dr. Thomas Henyey, the program's director and a geology professor at the University of Southern California, said, "We've been slow to realize that the earthquake hazard in Southern California involves more than the San Andreas fault." The fault traverses unpopulated areas east and north of Los Angeles. While the San Andreas is expected to produce a devastating magnitude-eight earthquake in coming years, he said, the Los Angeles basin lies over a convergence zone—a complicated geologic region that could produce a smaller but more damaging magnitude-seven earthquake in populated areas.

Not all earthquake experts agree that the buried faults are very dangerous.

"There's a certain amount of mob hysteria among scientists in Southern California," said Dr. Allan Lindh, chief seismologist at the United States Geological Survey in Menlo Park. "There are jillions of convergence zones with basins near them from Burma to Spain and no evidence that any of these has produced a magnitude-seven earthquake," he said. "The real threat to L.A. is the San Andreas. It's the difference of being hit by an asteroid or a car."

Beneath the layers of sedimentary rocks and thrust faults that scientists have been studying for some time lies a much deeper, horizontal fracture zone that geologists are just beginning to appreciate. Dr. Thomas Wright, a retired geologist from San Anselmo, California, and leading expert on the Los Angeles basin, said it is here that colder, harder rocks come into contact with warmer, softer rocks, forming a brittle-ductile transition. In the Los Angeles region, this area of basal detachment is nine miles down. The top zone of rocks is sliding over the lower zone like the top layer of a cake sliding over the lower layer.

Blind-thrust faults originate in that slowly sliding horizontal zone and form steep ramps that head toward the surface, Dr. Wright said. Each thrust fault is a segment of a larger system, riding a deep transition zone and being pushed along by the motions of the huge North American and Pacific crustal plates, which converge in California. Their boundary is the San Andreas fault.

Geologists argue about the angle, composition and motions of these blind-thrust faults, said Dr. Thomas Davis, an oil consultant from Valencia, California, who has mapped many of them.

Three major thrust-fault systems are currently being mapped, he said. The huge Elysian fault begins offshore, where it rises under the Channel Islands, traverses Santa Monica and pushes up the Santa Monica Mountains, and crosses into West Los Angeles and Hollywood, where it gives rise to Beverly Hills and the Hollywood Hills. It continues under the downtown area and forms the hill where Dodger Stadium sits, and goes on east through Whittier, Monterey Park and La Hacienda Heights, giving form to the Puente Hills and Coyote Hills, and ending around Chino. The top edge of the fault is about three miles below the surface, Dr. Davis said.

A second system lies beneath the Palos Verde peninsula and may extend out to San Nicholas Island, he said.

A third ramp pushes up under the San Gabriel Mountains, forming the Sierra Madre fault system all along the local foothills. This region has produced moderate earthquakes every couple of years since 1985 and is considered currently active.

Scientists use a variety of tools to characterize and map these blind-thrust faults. At Princeton University, Dr. John Suppe pioneered a method for inferring thrust-fault geometry based on surface-fold geometry. He looks at the shape of the folds and backtracks to determine what kind of deformation it took to create the folds. From that, he can calculate the depth, dip and size of ramps.

The method works well when the folds are relatively undisturbed, as they are throughout the coast ranges of central California, Dr. Suppe said. But in Los Angeles, the folds are often buried under sediments and topped with pavement.

Other researchers are applying advanced geodetic surveys to determine if the faults are locked or moving. Geodesy is a branch of mathematics that determines exact points on the Earth's surface and from them calculates the shape and movements of large areas of land, correcting for variations in gravity and magnetism.

This technique takes advantage of Department of Defense satellites, at least four of which are flying overhead at any one time, said Dr. Kenneth Hudnut, a geophysicist at the geological survey office in Pasadena. Their exact positions, along with a distant quasar, can be used to determine precise points on the Earth's surface with sublime accuracy.

To find out how much compression is occurring across the Los Angeles basin, Dr. Hudnut conscripts county surveyors to lay down special receivers as they go about their work mapping roads and property lines. Their signals are bounced off satellites and their positions calculated, allowing Dr. Hudnut to assemble a regional picture of fault motion and mountain building.

It will take another five years of data collection to measure possible slip rates on the faults, Dr. Hudnut said, but preliminary results indicate that the Los Angeles basin is closing up at a rate of about seven millimeters, or about a quarter of an inch, a year. Strain could be accumulating on one or many faults, he said, or the whole region could be slipping slowly and quietly.

In the meantime, geologists are scrutinizing Los Angeles neighborhoods for clues about past earthquakes. Although thrust faults do not break the surface, they leave disturbances that tell a story.

"There is a very pronounced scarp at University High School in West Los Angeles," Dr. Wright said. "If you stand on the south edge of the athletic field and look across, the academic buildings are forty to fifty feet above the field on this uplifted scarp. It's spooky."

The cliff at Pacific Palisades shows the trace of one thrust fault that may splay off a deeper one, Dr. Wright said. "These faults are not always blind," he said. "Sometimes the geologists are blind."

Dr. Davis and his partner, Jay Namson, are using data from past oil-well explorations in the Los Angeles region to construct models of blind-thrust faults. Oil pockets are often found under thrusts, Dr. Davis said, and natural oil seeps, like those found along the Malibu pier, indicate that faults are present.

Other scientists, like Dr. James Dolan of the California Institute of Technology, are taking a more direct approach. They examine open trenches to look for clues about past earthquakes. They map sediments, collect charcoal for dating soils and look for evidence of past movements.

Dr. Dolan stays in close touch with county and city crews who are digging storm drains and sewer lines across fault zones.

Preliminary results from these paleoseismological studies show that the Hollywood and Santa Monica faults do not move for thousands of years between earthquakes, while segments of the San Andreas fault break every few hundred years. But when rare earthquakes do occur on these blind thrusts, they might be very large.

Until the blind-thrust faults are assessed, Dr. Henyey said, scientists cannot give much advice to disaster-preparedness officials about what to expect from earthquakes in Los Angeles's basement. But based on the be-havior of similar faults, residents may want to batten down the hatches.

—SANDRA BLAKESLEE, August 1993

Hopes for Predicting Earthquakes, Once So Bright, Are Growing Dim

THE SCIENCE OF EARTHQUAKE PREDICTION has fallen on hard times.

Many of the nation's leading seismologists now think that earthquakes are inherently unpredictable. They say that the search for ways to warn people days, hours or minutes before an earthquake appears to be futile.

The only glimmer of hope offers little comfort. While recent research suggests that some earthquakes may produce precursory signals involving shifts in the Earth's crust, those signals are so small, faint and hidden from view that detecting them in any practical sense may be impossible.

A sense of earlier optimism has turned to pessimism, said Dr. Thomas Heaton, a seismologist at the United States Geological Survey in Pasadena, California. Moreover, such sentiments have important practical and political implications.

If earthquakes cannot be predicted, Dr. Heaton said, how should the $100 million now spent each year on earthquake research and hazard reduction be used? Currently, a third of that money is spent on finding ways to construct safer buildings, bridges and highways. The rest is spent on basic research on understanding earthquakes and looking for ways to predict them. Some scientists think that much more of the money should be spent on reducing the hazards, Dr. Heaton said.

Whatever is decided, earthquake prediction has undergone a reversal of fortune. From the 1960s through the mid-1980s, many scientists felt it could be done, said Dr. Thomas H. Jordan, a geophysicist at the Massachusetts Institute of Technology. In 1975, Chinese officials noted a rise in water table levels and predicted a major earthquake in the city of Haicheng, saving thousands of lives. The hope was that such warning signals would be typical of earthquakes, Dr. Jordan said. In 1976, the National Academy of Sciences issued a report, "Predicting Earthquakes," which argued that such efforts should be undertaken.

Two scientific models drove the optimism, Dr. Jordan said. One, called dilatancy theory, he said, is similar to what happens when people go out on a beach and step in wet sand and the sand gets dry around their feet. "The sand grains have been rotated and don't fit together as well," he explained, "decreasing their pore pressure and letting the water escape." People thought the same phenomenon would be observable in earthquake faults before their failure. Stressed rocks would deform in a characteristic way and release water that could be detected.

But aside from Haicheng, which was based on anecdotal reports, dilatancy has never been observed before an earthquake, Dr. Jordan said, and it was later shown that the idea would not work.

A second related idea, called the seismic gap hypothesis, says that earthquakes tend to repeat along known fault zones. After an earthquake, stress is released. But over time—usually several hundred years—strain reaccumulates and the fault is destined to break again in a more or less characteristic pattern. This model has been used to predict the likelihood of earthquakes reoccurring along a dozen segments of California's San Andreas fault. But those predictions are stated in decades rather than hours or minutes.

This optimism led to the creation of two major earthquake prediction experiments, Dr. Jordan said. Japanese scientists deployed an array of instruments along the Tokai fault near Tokyo. American scientists set instruments along a segment of the San Andreas fault in Parkfield, about half way between San Francisco and Los Angeles, where the seismic gap hypothesis predicted another earthquake should occur.

The instruments are designed to find precursors, like subtle motions in the Earth's crust, so that people can be warned shortly before an earthquake strikes, Dr. Jordan said.

But things have not been going as planned. The Parkfield earthquake is overdue; it was supposed to have happened by 1992. The most recent damaging earthquakes in America and Japan—Loma Prieta, Northridge and Kobe—struck without any precursory signals.

But more important, there has been a shift in thinking about the dynamics of earthquakes, Dr. Heaton said. The argument that big stresses build up along fault zones and then have to be released in a characteristic manner "doesn't make much sense," he said. Actual measurements deep in the ground indicate that stress within faults is pretty weak. "The mystery is why quakes occur at all with such small stresses," he said.

Clues are being found in the new science of chaos and complexity, Dr. Heaton said. Earthquakes are a classic example of a chaotic system, he said.

In this view, the Earth's crust—especially along fault zones—is prone to constant shifting. Tiny earthquakes are happening all the time. In California, scientists detect 25,000 to 50,000 earthquakes each year, Dr. Heaton said, most of which are not felt.

But for reasons that are not well understood, these small earthquakes sometimes do not stop. Local rock conditions or other geologic factors allow a magnitude-one earthquake to expand into a magnitude-two earthquake, involving a larger region. Less commonly, Dr. Heaton said, a magnitude-two earthquake sets off a magnitude-three earthquake and so on up the scale of earthshaking power.

"A big earthquake is simply a small one that ran away," Dr. Heaton said. A devastating magnitude-eight earthquake is set off by an ordinary twitch in the Earth's crust, according to this view. The problem, Dr. Heaton said, is "we might never be able to predict in detail which of the small quakes will become large."

While many scientists share this pessimism, Dr. Gregory Beroza and Dr. William Ellsworth, geophysicists at the Geological Survey office in Menlo Park, California, recently proposed an earthquake model that could provide a way of knowing which earthquakes are destined to be large.

"Before an earthquake happens, before you get sudden slipping on a fault, there is a slow steady slip, so slow that it does not generate seismic waves," Dr. Beroza said.

Such movement may continue for a year or more before it reaches a critical point where it gets hung up, Dr. Elllsworth said. It can then make the transition into high-speed slip—otherwise known as an earthquake.

By studying records of activity from many earthquakes within seconds before they slip, the two researchers found that larger earthquakes were preceded by slow slippage over larger areas. While a small earthquake might exhibit slow slippage over an area a few yards wide, a larger earthquake could involve an area several miles wide. Thus, in principle, it might be easier to detect large slow slipping regions than minuscule ones.

The question is whether scientists can find ways to detect slow slippage over larger areas. At this point, it is not practical, Dr. Ellsworth said. The slipping may be so trivial, slow or deeply buried in the Earth that it will be virtually impossible to detect.

After several recent earthquakes in California, researchers looked for signals of increased strain, suggesting slow slippage, and did not find it, Dr. Jordan said.

But in a "bitter irony," Dr. Heaton said, two years ago instruments detected slow slippage along a segment of the San Andreas fault near San Juan Batista. "It was a fabulous precursor," he said. "It was the perfect event for predicting a quake. And then nothing happened."

There could be other manifestations of slow slippage, Dr. Jordan said. Some scientists are hoping that mysterious magnetic signals, detected before the Loma Prieta earthquake, might be a reliable precursor to major earthquakes. And it is possible that some but not all earthquakes might be preceded by changes in water-table levels, water chemistry and radon gas escaping from wells.

Japanese researchers reported that increased levels of chloride and sulfate ions had been found in mineral water around Kobe in the four months before the earthquake there. And radon, a radioactive gas formed naturally by the breakdown of radium, had increased tenfold in the region's underground water from October to late December 1994. Nevertheless, such changes do not precede all earthquakes and cannot be used as a basis for issuing warnings to the public.

The debate about predicting earthquakes might normally remain in academic circles but for recent destructive earthquakes in California and Japan. Some people are calling for the government to stop spending money on earthquake research and put it all into reducing hazards, Dr. Jordan said, "but that would be foolish." Faults could interact in complex ways and not understanding them could be more costly in the long run.

Nevertheless, more could be spent on engineering research, Dr. Heaton said. "As a society we are seriously underinvesting in our knowledge of how buildings work in quakes, how the ground moves and how buildings react," he said. "Using current technique, earthquakes can cause severe damage to tall structures in our cities."

As president of the Seismological Society of America, Dr. Heaton has called for a moratorium on building any new structures over six stories high in the Los Angeles area. Recalling the aftermath of the Northridge earthquake, he said, "The corner 7-Elevens stood up fine.

"Maybe we should build more of those for office space than the vanity high-rises," at least until engineers know how to build tall structures that can withstand moderate and severe shaking, he said.

—SANDRA BLAKESLEE, August 1995

Bolivia Shakes, and So Does Theory on Deep Quakes

EXPERTS THOUGHT THEY HAD A pretty good idea of what caused deep earthquakes. These upheavals, which occur 200 to 400 miles below the Earth's surface, are puzzling in that they ought to be impossible. The pressures and temperatures at that depth are so great that rock should undergo no frictional sliding, the mechanism of garden-variety earthquakes near the surface. So most geologists came to believe that the crushing pressures and increasing heat below a certain depth squeezed the rock into forms that were suddenly denser, creating huge cracks that developed into big temblors.

No more. An extraordinarily big earthquake 395 miles beneath Bolivia not only shattered records by jolting cities as far away as Toronto but also left the squeeze theory shaken.

An analysis of shock waves from that earthquake show its fault zone was 30 miles long and 20 miles wide, too big to be explained by the leading theory. In fact, experts say, the quake bears a disturbing resemblance to big ones that occur near the Earth's surface.

"It's embarrassing," said Dr. Paul G. Silver, a geologist at the Carnegie Institution of Washington who questions the old theory. "It looks and acts and talks like these shallow earthquakes. But it shouldn't exist."

In place of the squeeze theory, Dr. Silver and his colleagues are proposing a new one that they say better fits evidence gathered by global arrays of detectors that track subtle ground motions over great distances.

But a main author of the old theory says it is still alive, although perhaps wounded, and can be repaired by taking the recent evidence into account.

"Even if they're right about the size of the faulting, it's not dead," said Dr. Harry W. Green II, a geologist at the University of California at Riverside. "Death knell is their favorite term. But that's grossly overblown."

No matter who wins the intellectual battle, experts agree that deep earthquakes are a general expression of plate tectonics. According to this theory, the slow churning of the Earth's hot interior constantly creates and moves big crustal plates. New crust is formed volcanically at long mid-ocean ridges, spreads across the sea floor, and is eventually destroyed hundreds or thousands of miles away as the cooling plate sinks beneath thick terrestrial plates and plunges headlong into the heart of the Earth.

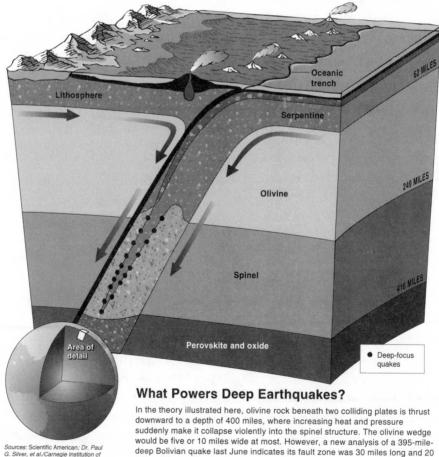

Lithosphere

Oceanic trench

62 MILES

Serpentine

Olivine

249 MILES

Spinel

416 MILES

Perovskite and oxide

Area of detail

● Deep-focus quakes

Sources: Scientific American; Dr. Paul G. Silver, et al./Carnegie Institution of Washington

What Powers Deep Earthquakes?

In the theory illustrated here, olivine rock beneath two colliding plates is thrust downward to a depth of 400 miles, where increasing heat and pressure suddenly make it collapse violently into the spinel structure. The olivine wedge would be five or 10 miles wide at most. However, a new analysis of a 395-mile-deep Bolivian quake last June indicates its fault zone was 30 miles long and 20 miles wide, casting the theory into doubt.

N.Y. Times News Service

The sinking process is known as "subduction" and is clearly the engine of deep earthquakes, as revealed by the fact that deep quakes occur only where one plate plunges beneath another, fated to melt in the Earth's hot interior.

The mystery is how earthquakes happen at all at remote depths where temperatures may exceed 2,900 degrees Fahrenheit and pressures are 240,000 times greater than those at the surface of the Earth. In theory, any rock there should have the consistency of putty, ruling out the brittle fracture and frictional sliding found in faults near the surface.

This paradox has been one of the main problems of geophysics ever since the remarkable depth of some earthquakes was first recognized seven decades ago.

A tentative answer began to emerge over the last decade. It centered on the idea that materials undergo phase transitions, as when liquid water turns into ice or graphite deep in the Earth's interior turns into diamonds.

The rocky material in a descending slab of subducted plate, scientists reasoned, might undergo phase transitions that left it suddenly denser, as diamond is denser than graphite. The atoms of the slab were simply repackaged in a closer form. And deep quakes were seen as a result of such rapid compactions.

The candidate material in this process was olivine, a predominant mineral in the descending plate. At a depth greater than 200 miles or so, it was seen as slowly transforming into a denser structure known as spinel. According to the quake theory, some olivine at the heart of relatively cool descending plates persisted much deeper, to depths as great as 400 miles, where increasing heat and pressure suddenly made it collapse into the spinel structure amid a great seismic disturbance.

The olivine wedge that could undergo such a fracture, scientists estimated, would at most be five or 10 miles wide.

Such reasoning got a major boost when Dr. Green of the University of California and his colleagues showed in a series of careful laboratory experiments that olivine under great pressure and heat formed cracks of high-density spinel. The cracking was totally different from the type that occurred in rock at the surface, but it was very real and was seen as the long-sought answer to the deep-quake riddle.

"Questions remain," Dr. Green wrote in *Scientific American* in 1994, "but the essential paradox behind deep earthquakes has been resolved."

Then came the new evidence that rattled the theory. The first sign of trouble was a big earthquake some 350 miles beneath the Tonga Islands in the South Pacific in March 1994. Analysis showed that its fault zone was 40 miles long and 30 miles wide. It was the first evidence of the dimensions of a deep fault and the first suggestion that a fault so deep could be so large.

The possibility that the Tonga reading was false or a fluke has now been dealt a blow by a new analysis of the big Bolivian quake, which occurred in June of 1994 at a depth of 395 miles. It hit where the Nazca oceanic plate slowly grinds its way beneath the western edge of South America.

Dr. Silver of the Carnegie Institution, along with six colleagues from Carnegie and the University of Arizona, reported in *Science* magazine that its fault zone was 30 miles long and 20 miles wide.

For both Tonga and Bolivia, the calculated fracture zone is far too big for the wedge cracking of the phase-transition theory.

Alternatively, Dr. Silver and his colleagues suggest that these large breakages may be caused by old faults and zones of weakness in the descending crustal slab, noting similarities between the deep Bolivian quake and the largest shallow ones.

"The hypothesis that deep events occur on preexisting faults," they wrote, "addresses perhaps the most intriguing and paradoxical feature of deep-focus events, namely their striking resemblance to earthquakes near the Earth's surface."

Staunchly defending the old theory, Dr. Green says the new analysis and the new theory are riddled with flawed assumptions. "The arguments they make are great for headlines, but they don't go very far," he said in an interview.

For instance, he said size estimates of the faults were based on complex interpretative aids and could be wrong. Or the faulting in the olivine could be occurring in parallel bars across the wedge, as some evidence seems to suggest.

"There are half a dozen different ways out of this," he said of the assault. "If there are questions from this earthquake, we can go back and ask questions and see what needs to be modified. The question is whether this is really a big problem or whether the theory just needs some refinement."

Dr. Seth Stein, a geologist at Northwestern University outside Chicago who has followed the dispute, which was first aired at a meeting of the American Geophysical Union, said that while the Bolivian event posed a sharp challenge to the old theory, it was not necessarily a fatal one.

"It's a very serious problem for the hypothesis," he said in an interview. "Silver's observations are terribly important. But I suspect the problem is in our models of the slabs rather than our thinking about the mechanism of the earthquake. The slab simply has to be more complex than we've been thinking."

Dr. Silver agreed with that possibility in an interview, noting that the new model suggested that slab imperfections were the long-sought explanation for the deep earthquakes. He also said the new seismic evidence was destined to lay the old theory to rest.

"I think it's going to be very difficult to get out of," he said of the Bolivian data.

—WILLIAM J. BROAD, April 1995

Theory of Plate Movement Marks Zones That Breed Frequent Quakes

GEOLOGISTS HAVE KNOWN FOR DECADES about the cause of most of the planet's earthquakes, strings of blockbusters that release more than 80 percent of the destructive energy that shakes the Earth. These convulsive jolts occur as the dozen or so ambulatory slabs that make up the surface grind past one another. Deep in the Earth, this movement stores up stress energies that periodically explode along rocky fault lines to level cities and cleave mountains.

The mystery has been why some plate movements produce so many earthquakes and others cause very few or none at all—an enigma of no small importance to the millions of people who live near earthquake zones and are eager to know the probabilities of future calamities.

Now a pair of scientists from the United States and Chile have come up with what appears to be the answer. In a theory of surprising simplicity, they propose that the descending rims of plates act as hidden switches to turn great earthquakes on and off. The switch is on when the rim of one plate is pressed hard against another, increasing friction, and is off in the opposite position. The switch's position, they add, is determined by whether the plates are colliding (on) or moving in the same general direction (off).

The finding, reported in *The Journal of Geophysical Research,* not only explains the locations of most past earthquakes but also forecasts where new ones will occur. One predicted danger zone is in Oregon and Washington, a relatively quiescent area where warnings about the potential of huge quakes have risen steadily in recent years.

"The Cascadia area comes up as being one of the most compressive regions, right up there with Chile," said Dr. Christopher H. Scholz, an

On-Off Switch for Earthquakes

The earthquake switch is on when the descending rim of one plate is pressed hard against another, increasing friction and quakes. The switch is off when the rim is pulled sharply down and friction with the opposing plate is reduced.

Switch on; plates move in opposite directions.

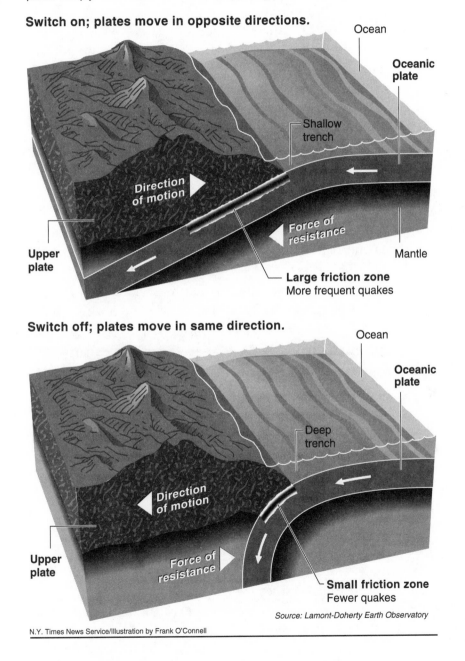

Ocean

Oceanic plate

Shallow trench

Direction of motion

Force of resistance

Mantle

Upper plate

Large friction zone
More frequent quakes

Switch off; plates move in same direction.

Ocean

Oceanic plate

Deep trench

Direction of motion

Force of resistance

Upper plate

Small friction zone
Fewer quakes

Source: Lamont-Doherty Earth Observatory

N.Y. Times News Service/Illustration by Frank O'Connell

author of the new theory and a geophysicist at Lamont-Doherty, the Earth sciences research institute of Columbia University. "That's where we're waiting for one, in places like Seattle."

The other author of the report is Dr. Jaime Campos, a seismologist at the University of Chile in Santiago.

Many scientists applaud the study and say it advances the field of quake theoretics to a significant new stage. But many also caution that the proposed mechanisms still have to be verified.

"At a minimum, it's a significant quantitative step," said Dr. Larry Ruff of the University of Michigan, a leader in the field. "It could be they've put it all together."

Dr. Hiroo Kanamori, a seismologist at the California Institute of Technology who pioneered the study of the great earthquake zones, said only time would tell how well the theory fit all the evidence.

"All the studies to date are empirical," Dr. Kanamori said in an interview. "No one has studied the mechanism. This paper goes the furthest in terms of physical mechanism, and that's an important step. But whether it's right or wrong, we'll have to see."

The theory of plate tectonics says the Earth's surface is made up of a dozen or so big crustal slabs that float on a sea of molten rock. Over the ages, the slow churning of this inner sea constantly moves these plates as well as their superimposed continents, which are torn apart and re-arranged like pieces of a jigsaw puzzle.

The plates move like conveyor belts. New plate material is ejected volcanically at long midocean ridges. From there it spreads out across the ocean floor and is eventually destroyed hundreds or thousands of miles away as the cooling slab collides with and then sinks beneath other plates, plunging headlong back into the hot Earth for recycling. The sinking process is known as subduction.

Subduction zones are the globe's earthquake hot spots, accounting for more than 80 percent of all the seismic energy released on Earth. They also produce the really big upsets, ones far bigger than underground nuclear explosions. Such convulsions include the magnitude-nine earthquake that struck Alaska in 1964 and produced widespread ruin.

Other subduction zones with blockbuster earthquakes are found off Japan, western Mexico, Chile, western South America in general and many deep-ocean trenches in the western Pacific. The earthquake that leveled parts of the city of Kobe, Japan, was linked to plate subduction offshore.

As the plate tectonic theory emerged in the 1960s and 1970s, and as global studies of seismicity improved, scientists became more and more aware of seismic quiet zones where few or no quakes occurred, even though these areas were apparently subducting and tectonic theory predicted they should be boiling with destructive energy. Such areas include places where the Pacific slab hits the Philippine slab, forming deep trenches beneath the sea.

As such data emerged, many scientists tried to explain the silence, including Dr. Kanamori of Caltech, Dr. Ruff of the University of Michigan and Dr. Seiya Uyeda of Tokia University in Japan. One observation was that plates in head-to-head collision had a greater chance of earthquakes, though no one could explain why that should be so in terms of a physical mechanism. Some scientists suggested that subduction occurred in episodic bursts rather than continuously, while others said perhaps the differing age of plates explained the riddle.

Then a big earthquake struck Guam in 1993, damaging hotels, touching off landslides, throwing cars off bridges and knocking out communications as telephone poles toppled. Its size was measured as 7.8 on the Richter scale of ground motion. In contrast, the San Francisco earthquake of 1906 was estimated at 8.2 on the Richter scale.

The Guam quake caught the eye of many scientists, including Dr. Scholz of Lamont-Doherty, because in theory it should not have happened. Guam is at an intersection of the Pacific and Philippine plates where plate boundaries are uncertain and where subduction seems to be minimal and earthquakes are infrequent.

"It was a big clue," Dr. Scholz recalled. "The area was suppose to have almost no earthquakes. And suddenly it had this big one. That made things quite intriguing."

The area became a focus for his theoretical investigations. He worked on the problem with Dr. Campos. At the time, both scientists were at the Institute de Physique du Globe in Paris. The team considered the Pacific area under study ideal because the Pacific plate was clearly of uniform age, eliminating the possibility that different ages and levels of cooling accounted for the seismic differences.

What the scientists found was that when an oceanic slab meets another and bends down into the hot and relatively soft mantle below, it does so at a shallow angle if the two plates are moving toward each other, but at a steep angle if they are moving in the same general direction over the underlying mantle.

The angle of descent determines the likelihood of a great quake, with shallow angles producing much friction between plates and thus much seismic shaking. Steep angles produce much less rubbing between the plates, and thus no great quakes.

According to the scientists, the angle of plate descent is determined by forces acting on the descending plate as it moves through the mantle. When the upper of two intersecting plates moves over the mantle toward the descending one, then the downward-going slab is forced to move through the mantle at a shallow angle. But when two plates travel in the same direction over the mantle, resistive forces in the mantle push against the descending slab and bend it down sharply.

"It's like moving your finger through a honey jar," Dr. Scholz said of the slab moving through the mantle. "It resists."

In their work, the scientists applied their model to the subduction zone between the Pacific and Philippine plates and explained to their satisfaction the observed quake activity along the great arc of ocean trenches that sweep the western Pacific. These trenches, produced by the forces of subduction, are named Marianas, Bonin and Izu and run from north of New Guinea up to Japan.

In their analysis, more earthquakes should have rocked Guam than seemed to occur, since the nearby descending plate went down at a shallow angle. To their delight, they discovered old records kept by Catholic priests that revealed that the Guam region actually danced with big convulsions over the centuries.

The two then applied their model to the rest of the globe, finding that it explained more than 80 percent of the earthquakes (or lack of them) in the world's 29 subduction zones. Ten percent of the zones had physical complications like multiple plate intersections that were beyond the model's explanatory powers. The other 10 percent remain a mystery.

For the United States, the model predicts that the Juan de Fuca plate slowly subducting under the North American plate is going down at a shallow angle and is capable of generating earthquakes greater than a magnitude of eight. That is considered quite large and capable of producing major damage and loss of life if it strikes near a city.

Oregon, Washington and Northern California have suffered no great quakes in historical times, Dr. Scholz noted, but that discrepancy may simply be due to the fact that the intervals between them in this region are stretched out longer than in others.

The scientific reactions to the theory so far, Dr. Scholz said, tend to be: "That's so obvious. Why didn't I think of it?"

—WILLIAM J. BROAD, November 1995

3

STORMS AND HURRICANES

Earthquakes and volcanoes are fortunately rare, but the weather is often disturbed in one way or another. On occasion these disturbances assume highly destructive forms, such as tornadoes and hurricanes. Tornadoes are hard to forecast, but hurricanes are one of the few natural disasters that can now be predicted well enough to avoid the substantial loss of life they once caused.

Hurricanes develop out at sea and are tracked by weather satellites. Forecasts of their course and ferocity have enough credibility that people take evacuation orders seriously.

But though the human toll from hurricanes is much less, damage to property has steadily risen and will continue to do so. The reason is that people like to live near the sea, and the coastal areas of the United States are becoming increasingly built up. Hurricane Andrew in 1992 caused only 50 deaths but more than $30 billion in property damage. Forecasters say it is only a matter of time before the United States experiences a $50 billion hurricane.

Weather experts believe that starting in 1995 a phase of more intense hurricanes has begun, though they differ on whether this has anything to do with the global warming of the climate. The storms known as northeasters, which are a whirl of winds like hurricanes but can form over land as well as sea, also seem to be intensifying.

Hurricanes pack winds that range from 74 up to 160 miles an hour and can last for two weeks. Their most destructive component, however, is often not the winds but the storm surge, a dome of raised water that may be up to 20 feet high and extend for miles.

The winds of tornadoes run from 73 to 318 miles an hour. The strongest tornadoes can lift homes off their foundations and toss cars as far as 100 yards.

Radar Peeks at Structure
Hidden Inside Tornado

THE TERRIFYING SIGHT OF A twister funnel roaring down a highway and peeling off the asphalt pavement like so much dead skin is enough to send sensible drivers scurrying to safety.

But by driving their truck almost into the teeth of tornadoes and probing them with pencil-thin radar beams, a team of scientists has begun to reveal the complex air structures that control the behavior of these deadly storms.

These are not the fictional tornado chasers of the movie *Twister.* Dr. Joshua Wurman and Dr. Jerry M. Straka of the University of Oklahoma and Dr. Erik N. Rasmussen of the National Severe Storms Laboratory in Norman, Oklahoma, are genuine. And they claim to have recorded the closest fine-scale radar soundings ever made of a tornado. In a paper published in the journal *Science,* they report their measurements of a violent tornado that swept across the Texas panhandle near Dimmitt on June 3, 1995.

The scientists managed to maneuver their truck-mounted radar apparatus to a little less than two miles from the center of the funnel and probed the storm's winds for 12 minutes. As they did so, the twister, with winds of more than 160 miles an hour, destroyed a house, picked up cars and hurled them 600 feet and stripped the pavement from a 130-foot stretch of road as it crossed.

"We can always outrun a tornado," Dr. Wurman said in an interview, "and in case our old truck should stall at an inconvenient moment, we generally have a backup car behind us. The real danger is of traffic accidents caused by local tornado fans who often follow us when they spot our flashing lights."

The Tilt That Makes a Tornado

In an ordinary thunderstorm warm air rises straight up. Rain then develops directly over the rising air, and as it falls through cools the air, halting the upward flow. But, in some other storms wind shear tilts the cell so rainfall misses the main body of rising air and allows an updraft to continue. Scientists say this air movement can give rise to a tornado.

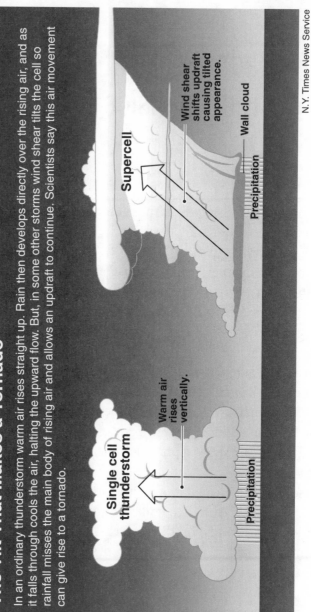

Single cell thunderstorm

Warm air rises vertically.

Precipitation

Supercell

Wind shear shifts updraft causing tilted appearance.

Wall cloud

Precipitation

N.Y. Times News Service

Tornado research conducted by the Norman group has no immediate application to weather forecasting, and the scientists do not work with the National Weather Service. But ultimately they hope to gather enough data on the transition of certain types of thunderstorms into full-fledged tornadoes that people in the paths of such storms can be warned earlier than is now possible.

"At present no one understands why it is that the same type of thunderstorm sometimes spawns a tornado and sometimes does not," Dr. Wurman said. "But with greater knowledge, we may one day be able to lengthen warning times from, say, five minutes to fifteen minutes. That margin could save lives by giving people a little more time to run to storm cellars."

The heart of the team's apparatus is a Doppler radar system assembled from a military-surplus parabolic antenna six feet in diameter and an old transmitter acquired from the National Center for Atmospheric Research in Boulder, Colorado. The reflection of a thin Doppler radar beam reveals not only the position and shape of a target, but also the target's relative speed as it approaches or recedes. With a beam as thin as the one used by Dr. Wurman's group, it is possible to form images of the small-scale features of a tornado, including the paths of its swirling winds, its powerful up and down drafts and the shearing of air moving at different speeds.

Dry air does not usually reflect enough radar to be detected, but within a tornado, churning air currents contain rain drops, hail and debris ranging in size from dust grains to entire houses; all of these objects reflect radar and can reveal the contours and behavior of the storm winds that carry them. Even relatively empty air masses may contain clouds of insects that provide reflective targets for radar beams.

Sometimes masses of dry air alone may contain discontinuities of temperature and density that slightly reflect radar, Dr. Wurman said, but such features are only weakly reflective and are difficult to detect.

The analysis Dr. Wurman and his colleagues made of radar data from the 1995 tornado near Dimmitt revealed a very complex structure that confirmed some of the models proposed by theorists. Features included unexpected spiraling bands of differing radar reflectivity, intense wind-shear zones, debris "shields" corresponding to cylindrical layers of wind, the storm's calm "eye," and occasional protrusions of wind jets into the eye.

The group found evidence of a phenomenon that had been surmised but never demonstrated: that at least some tornadoes embody a central shaft of downward-moving air sheathed by a cone-shaped funnel spiraling upward. A tornado sucks huge volumes of air and material from the ground surface and carries them aloft, and some of the air supplied to this spinning chimney apparently comes from a central downdraft.

The wind speeds in a tornado are highest a few hundred feet above the ground, not at ground level itself, Dr. Wurman said. The reason is that the ground offers frictional resistance to the winds in direct contact with it.

Although Dr. Wurman and his colleagues race around "Tornado Alley" in their truck searching for twisters in a region covering Oklahoma and parts of a half dozen neighboring states, they have yet to catch a fetal tornado before it is born. Tornadoes are born suddenly and leave little time for observation and measurements; some tornadoes last up to an hour, but many others survive no longer than a few minutes.

"There are many theoretical models describing how tornadoes form, but predictions based on these models are often contradictory," Dr. Wurman said. "By getting close-up, high-resolution radar images of air circulation within the storms themselves, we may be able to remove some of the uncertainties."

Dr. Wurman said the team has come close. They spotted a tornado in Oklahoma just as it was forming and they were able to track its development as a large twister, one in which the 80-mile-an-hour winds around the funnel were as strong as the winds in the funnel itself.

It seems, Dr. Wurman said, that tornadoes are spawned by special storms called "super-cell thunderstorms," in which a peculiar hooked cloud often signals an incipient tornado. When a tornado forms, it develops from the tip of this hook.

In an ordinary thunderstorm, he said, warm air creates a convection cell that rises more or less vertically. Rain then develops directly over the cell, and as it falls through the cell it cools the air, halting the upward flow. But in some other storms, Dr. Wurman said, wind shear tilts the normally vertical cell so rain falling above its upper end misses the main body of the cell. This can give rise to a "super cell" that sometimes spawns a tornado.

A surprise that the group encountered in the 1995 tornado was the discovery of a series of nested rings, or bands of radar reflectivity, surrounding the storm's eye. Their tentative explanation is that a tornado somehow sorts out particles of different masses—debris versus raindrops, for example—and arranges them in separate bands.

The group at the University of Oklahoma has acquired two trucks carrying radar equipment and plans to extend its operations. But the chances of finding and reaching a tornado before it dies are still small, and the scientists waste much time driving hundreds of miles in their daily searches.

They plan to augment their tornado-catching equipment with small devices capable of measuring air pressure, relative humidity and temperature. When a tornado has been spotted heading for a road, the team plans to drop 30 of these "ducks" at intervals along the road, so that the tornado must hit at least one of the little sensors.

"To give you an idea of the difficulty of tornado chasing," Dr. Wurman said, "we estimate that in Oklahoma's tornado belt, the probable frequency of a tornado passing within six miles of any given spot is only once in one hundred years. We have to be very lucky and very fast to reach a tornado in time.

"But we're getting better all the time."

—MALCOLM W. BROWNE, June 1996

Historic Hurricane Could Catch Northeast with Its Guard Down

SOONER OR LATER, METEOROLOGICAL CIRCUMSTANCES will conspire to hurl another storm as strong as the legendary hurricane of September 1938 against a complacent Northeastern United States, and its cost in lives and property could be the highest ever exacted by a hurricane in this country. Or so concludes a new analysis of past hurricane behavior and present Northeastern development.

Only sheer chance kept this from happening in 1985 and 1991, when Hurricanes Gloria and Bob, respectively, struck the Northeast, according to the author of the study, Dr. Nicholas K. Coch, a geologist at Queens College. Had either of those storms drifted into a certain meteorological "slot" as the 1938 hurricane did, it could well have been more catastrophic than Florida's 1992 disaster, Hurricane Andrew, the most destructive tropical storm ever to hit the United States mainland.

This would have been true, says Dr. Coch, even though Andrew was the much stronger and more intense storm. It was rated as a category 4 storm (with sustained winds of 131 to 155 miles an hour) on the Saffir-Simpson scale of hurricane intensity. Category 5 hurricanes, with winds above 155 miles an hour, are the strongest. They are never seen in the Northeast, because the cooler waters of the northern ocean impart less energy to the storm than the warm seas of the Tropics. Category 4 storms are considered only remotely possible in the Northeast. But if conditions are right, the 111-to-130-mile-an-hour winds whirling about the eye of a strong category 3 hurricane (the rating of both Gloria and Bob) could be boosted suddenly to category 4 strength by the extra jolt imparted by strong winds off the Northeast coast.

It happens this way:

The huricane, initially propelled westward by winds in the Tropics, travels around the western side of the big midocean mass of high-pressure air known as the "Bermuda high," and then drifts northward. Another high-pressure system over the Eastern United States acts in concert with the Bermuda high to create a north-south slot of low pressure into which the hurricane has no choice but to move.

As the storm moves north, the "steering winds" in which it is embedded become progressively stronger. When this increased wind speed is added to that of the counterclockwise winds on the eastern side of the hurricane itself, those east-side winds get a boost that elevates the storm, in effect, to category 4—just in time to drive it across some part of the New York metropolitan area.

The storm's increasing forward speed makes it more formidable in two other respects as well: it allows the hurricane to race across the cooler northern waters before they can weaken it too much, and the momentum enables the storm to punch its swath of destruction many miles inland.

The meteorological setup that makes all this possible, which occurs perhaps 10 times a year, hurricane or not, is precisely what developed as the 1938 hurricane approached Long Island on a course that eventually took it deep into New England. It turned a category 3 storm into what still ranks as the seventh most costly hurricane in United States history and the most disastrous ever recorded in the Northeast. Today, because 56 years' worth of development and population growth have expanded the possibilities for disaster enormously, and because Northeasterners have not experienced a truly big hurricane in decades and are largely unprepared, a similar storm could be far more catastrophic than Hurricane Andrew, Dr. Coch concluded.

While Dr. Coch's general analysis is correct, whether a northern hurricane would eclipse Andrew would depend largely on where in the metropolitan area the storm struck, said Brian Jarvinen, a research meteorologist at the National Hurricane Center in Coral Gables, Florida. The closer the storm's track was to New York, he said, the greater the damage would be. And while such a storm could develop in any given hurricane season, he said, "based on climatology you'd expect to see a hurricane in the region every twelve years" on average.

Dr. Coch has been purveying this message for some time, only to be received much like Cassandra, whose warnings of disaster were invariably greeted by disbelief. "We talk and we publish," he says, "but I've just about given up."

His latest publication on the subject is called "Hurricane Hazards Along the Northeastern Atlantic Coast of the United States." It appears in a book called *Coastal Hazards: Perception, Susceptibility and Mitigation*, published by the Coastal Education and Research Foundation in Charlottesville, Virginia.

In it, he identifies two accidents of geography that can conspire to help turn a middling-strong hurricane into a killer when it hits the Northeast. Both involve the angle formed by the north-south coast of New Jersey and the east-west coasts of Long Island and southern New England. When a northward-moving hurricane runs parallel to the coast, its weaker left side strikes the coast. But if and when it crosses Long Island—the most likely path, based on historical records—the full force of its stronger right side is brought to bear on areas east of the storm's eye. Unfortunately, as Dr. Coch writes, the Long Island shoreline "is the most densely populated and developed hurricane-prone coastal area in America."

Moreover, the storm drives a surge of sea water ahead of it. When the surge encounters the right angle made by the coast to form what is called the New York Bight, the water tends to pile up there as the hurricane gets closer. When the storm arrives, its rotating winds drive these waters against the New Jersey coast, into New York Harbor and against such places as Coney Island, Rockaway and Long Beach on Western Long Island. The surge on Long Island is heightened further by a wide, gently sloping portion of the continental shelf.

The disastrous northeasters of December 1992 and March 1993 provided a foretaste of the pattern of damage to be expected from this convergence of factors, Dr. Coch writes. But the severity of the damage could be much greater; the 1992 storm's maximum winds were equal only to those of a category 1 hurricane, and then only in gusts.

The "worst-case" scenario for the New York metropolitan area, Dr. Coch writes, would be a category 3 hurricane that bears inland across central New Jersey on a northwesterly track. In this case, the powerful right side of the hurricane would strike the metropolitan area squarely, according to the Coch paper, producing a storm surge of 20 feet in Raritan Bay and New York Harbor, 15 to 19 feet along highly urbanized parts of Brooklyn and Queens and 22 to 24 feet along the north side of Jamaica Bay in the communities of Howard Beach, Canarsie, Gerritsen Beach, Mill Basin and Flatlands.

This worst-case hurricane, said Mr. Jarvinen, could cause damages amounting to between $50 billion and $100 billion. By contrast, Hurricane Andrew's damages amounted to about $30 billion once all claims were settled.

Winds, especially the inevitable gusts that are stronger than the sustained winds that define a category 3 storm, would rip up trees, which in turn would drag down power lines. They would lift the roofs off houses and expose the interiors to heavy rain damage. They would strip the outer coverings off the upper stories of high-rise shoreline buildings and blow out their interiors, while the lower floors would be inundated by storm surge, according to the study. Dr. Coch notes that high-rise construction along the coasts of New York and New Jersey has never been tested by a major storm. The damage to high-rises inflicted by Hurricane Andrew "should be appreciated more" by this area's inhabitants, he writes.

Some scientists believe that the frequency of Atlantic hurricanes rises and falls in sequences of two decades or so. If so, a period of relatively less frequent hurricanes is nearing its end and a period of relatively more frequent ones is about to begin. If this belief is borne out and Dr. Coch's analysis is correct, the odds will rise on the prospect of more frequent category 3 hurricanes in the Northeast, and on their chances of encountering the conditions that would convert them into Andrew-size killers.

"Chance can easily make any one of them the next big one," Dr. Coch writes.

Should such a storm materialize, Dr. Coch says, its impact could be worsened by the region's lack of recent experience with a true monster hurricane. Since the area has not experienced one since 1938, lack of awareness would probably make the necessary evacuations more difficult, Dr. Coch concludes.

Increasing hurricane awareness is one measure that could help, he writes. Others include updating building codes to make structures more hurricane-resistant. (Mr. Jarvinen said that in southern Florida codes were designed to cope with storms of category 3 or less, that this was far from adequate to cope with Andrew and that codes in the Northeast are proba-

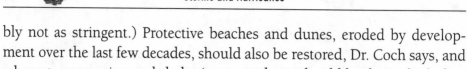

bly not as stringent.) Protective beaches and dunes, eroded by development over the last few decades, should also be restored, Dr. Coch says, and adequate evacuation and sheltering procedures should be devised—before the big one arrives.

But arrive it will, Dr. Coch says. The only question is when.

—WILLIAM K. STEVENS, August 1994

Fewer Northeasters Pound U.S., but Punch Is More Powerful

FOR PEOPLE WHO HAVE SUFFERED through the gales, heavy rains, floods, deep snows, property destruction and lost power of the nasty northeasters of the 1990s, there is little comfort in the fact that recent decades have seen fewer of these classic storms. That is because northeasters in general are more severe than they used to be.

The main reason, experts say, is a long-term shift in the predominant winter path of the North American jet stream—the high-altitude, west-to-east river of air in which counterclockwise spinning northeasters are born, from which they draw their energy and by which they are transported. The jet stream shift tends to throw large air masses together in a pattern that strengthens the storms. The northeaster that pounded New York in October 1996, as well as the previous January's blizzard, were variations on the main theme.

It is unclear whether the shift in large-scale atmospheric circulation that has brought more severe northeasters to the Middle Atlantic and New England states is a result of natural variation in the climate system or is related to changing global temperature patterns that accompany global warming.

"The outright honest answer is that we don't know" what is behind the change, said Dr. Robert E. Davis, a climatologist at the University of Virginia.

His own opinion, he said, is that the shift in circulation is from natural causes. Other experts say that while climatic change caused by heat-trapping industrial gases like carbon dioxide might be contributing, there is virtually no way to distinguish the human influence from natural factors.

Like the hurricane, the northeaster is a cyclone, meaning that its winds circulate counterclockwise around a center. But while hurricanes are born in warm tropical waters in the summer and early fall, northeasters originate as ordinary low-pressure systems in temperate latitudes in fall, winter and early spring. They typically form in one of seven places: near the Bahamas or north of Cuba; over or near Florida; in the Gulf of Mexico; along the Appalachians; off Cape Hatteras, North Carolina; off the mid-Atlantic Coast; and far inland, around Colorado. The jet stream transports them to the heavily populated Northeast.

Northeasters also wreak their havoc differently from hurricanes. While hurricanes are more tightly wound and have more powerful sustained winds, they affect a smaller area when they hit land; a northeaster, on the other hand, can ravage almost the entire coast. And while a hurricane can punch far inland and spin off tornadoes there, a northeaster's direct physical damage is usually limited to the coast. It causes damage mainly by sending high waves ashore over a long period, often several days.

Dr. Davis and a colleague at Virginia, Dr. Robert Dolan, have devised a scale for rating the severity of northeasters. Like the Saffir-Simpson scale for hurricanes, it classifies northeasters in five categories of intensity. The categories for northeasters are based on the combination of two factors: wave height and duration of the storm.

Using this classification system, Dr. Davis and Dr. Dolan have analyzed northeasters over the last half century and found that the strongest storms tend to occur in October, January and March. They have also found that from the mid-1940s through the mid-1960s, there were about 33 northeasters a year. This dropped to about 22 from the mid-1960s through the mid-1970s. Since then the frequency has varied but has not consistently reached pre-1965 levels.

But since the mid-1960s, the storms have generally been stronger. Research to date, say Dr. Davis and other researchers, implicates the shift in the jet stream as the cause. Instead of following a more or less straight path across the continent, the sinuous, constantly shifting jet has tended in recent decades to follow a curvier course, often dipping far to the south in the Eastern United States and offshore Atlantic, then turning northward along the coast.

In this pattern's most dangerous permutation, cold air to the west of the jet and warm ocean air to the east clash, and the sharp pressure difference between the two air masses creates strong winds around the rotating storm as the jet carries it northward. Further, a high-pressure system over New England or eastern Canada blocks the storm, allowing it to pound the coast for days at a time. The rotating storm typically hurls its winds from the northeast; hence, the northeaster.

There are a number of variations on this theme. The October 18 to 21 northeaster, for instance, was one in which the storm detached itself from the jet stream. Deprived of the jet's transport mechanism, it stalled and was blocked even more effectively by the typical high-pressure system over eastern Canada. At the same time, it drew extra moisture from nearby Hurricane Lili. This was largely responsible for the heavy rains that set records from New Jersey northward and that amounted to nearly 20 inches in some parts of Maine.

In another variation, the Halloween northeaster of 1991 merged with Hurricane Grace to produce a monster hundreds of miles wide that severely battered the Northeast with what Dr. Davis says were the highest waves in his 50-year record.

Yet another variation occurs when frigid arctic air moves in from Canada behind the southward-bulging jet stream and the storm is close enough to it for the rain to change to snow. The result can be blizzards like those of mid-March 1993, the so-called storm of the century, which affected everyone from the Deep South through New England, as well as the Northeast blizzard of January 1996, which set all-time records for snow depth.

While no one can predict how often northeasters will come and go in the future and how destructive they will be, Dr. Davis and Dr. Dolan point to an ominous human factor in the equation of damage. Writing in *American Scientist* three years ago, they warned, "As the population density along the Atlantic Coast continues to increase, northeasters will have an even greater impact upon the lives and livelihoods of coastal residents."

—WILLIAM K. STEVENS, October 1996

Storm Warning: Bigger Hurricanes and More of Them

THE EAST AND GULF COASTS OF the United States may be entering a long-anticipated, prolonged siege of more frequent and more destructive hurricanes, forecasters say.

They predict that more hurricanes than normal will develop in the tropical North Atlantic for the third straight year. This would make 1995 to 1997 the most active three-year period on record for the pinwheeling oceanic cyclones, and the experts say that could be only the beginning.

The 1970s, 1980s and early 1990s were a time of relatively infrequent hurricanes. Those years did have their big storms: seven of the 10 most costly hurricanes ever to strike the United States mainland did so over that stretch, including Hurricane Andrew in 1992, the costliest ever. But a federal study attributes the trend of escalating damage over that period to expanding population and exploding development rather than more frequent or powerful storms.

Now the atmosphere and ocean appear to have entered a new and more ominous hurricane phase. Some experts believe the turbulent stretch beginning in 1995 signifies a return to the 1940s, 1950s and 1960s, a period of high hurricane activity in the United States. If that is so, according to the federal study, the cost of damage wrought by hurricanes—already the most expensive natural disasters in America—could soar to new heights.

Scientists offer varying explanations of what is responsible for the increase in hurricane frequency. One study has found that sea-surface temperatures in 1995 were the highest on record in the tropical North Atlantic. That year, 19 tropical storms and hurricanes, double the 1946 to 1995 average, formed in the Atlantic. The authors of the study concluded that warmer seas encouraged incipient hurricanes to develop by infusing

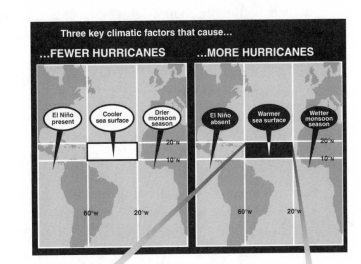

Three key climatic factors that cause...

...FEWER HURRICANES

...MORE HURRICANES

El Niño present

Cooler sea surface

Drier monsoon season

El Niño absent

Warmer sea surface

Wetter monsoon season

"A Deadly Threat Intensifies"

Citing a variety of climatic indicators, scientists fear an increase in Atlantic hurricanes over the next decade or two. An increase, if it occurs, could cause severe problems along the East Coast of the United States, much of which has been intensely developed during years of relative calm.

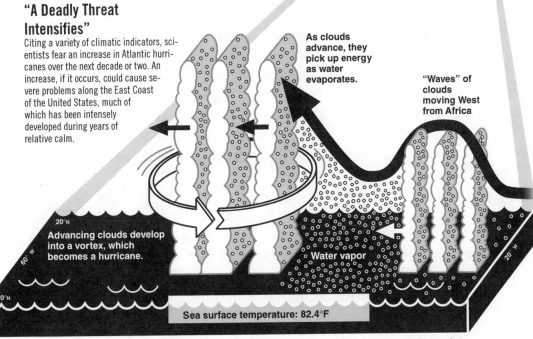

As clouds advance, they pick up energy as water evaporates.

"Waves" of clouds moving West from Africa

Advancing clouds develop into a vortex, which becomes a hurricane.

Water vapor

Sea surface temperature: 82.4°F

N.Y. Times News Service

them with more energy. Temperatures in the region of hurricane births, between 10 degrees and 20 degrees north latitude, have remained above average since 1995.

Coincidentally or not, 1995 also saw the highest average global surface temperatures on record, and some scientists say this raises the possibility that global warming is contributing to the increased frequency of hurricanes. The coincidence "is suggestive of some link to global warming, but that needs to be proved," said Dr. Mark A. Saunders, chief author of the study. It is "just one of the possibilities," he said.

Others say that global warming is almost certainly not the cause. One is Dr. William M. Gray, an atmospheric scientist and hurricane expert at Colorado State University in Fort Collins. The rise in sea temperature "is not related to the warming of the planet," he said, noting that global warming has been slow, while the Atlantic sea-surface temperature jumped in a matter of months.

It was Dr. Gray and his group of researchers who correctly predicted that 1995 would be one of the most active seasons on record, although they underestimated 1996. In April, the group forecast that 1997 would also bring more hurricanes than average, including the more intense ones. These major storms are defined as those with peak sustained winds of more than 110 miles an hour, and they account for 75 percent of all hurricane damage. Lesser hurricanes have peak winds of at least 74 miles an hour.

The forecasts are based on an array of predictive signs and atmospheric phenomena that Dr. Gray has identified as determining hurricane activity. One is the amount of rainfall in the Sahel region of western Africa, where the small areas of low pressure that are the embryos of hurricanes first form. When the Sahel is wetter, Dr. Gray found, more embryos form.

Another factor is the phenomenon known as El Niño, the huge pool of warm water that develops every two to seven years in the eastern tropical Pacific, changing weather patterns around the world. When it is in place, high-level winds blowing from the west tend to shear off the tops of developing hurricanes in the adjacent Atlantic, causing them to abort.

Other elements include the behavior of stratospheric winds that circle the globe high above the Equator and weather features far remote from the

Atlantic hurricane belt—things, for example, like the temperature high above Singapore.

One of the most powerful indicators, according to the study by Dr. Saunders and Andrew R. Harris, climate scientists at University College London in Britain, is the Atlantic sea-surface temperature. Their statistical analysis found that while most of the relevant factors were indeed favorable for hurricane development in the banner year of 1995, the dominating influence was the unusually warm ocean. The temperature in the region where hurricanes develop was 1.2 degrees Fahrenheit above the 1946 to 1995 average, a record. The development region was 0.36 of a degree warmer than average in 1996 and was about 0.9 of a degree warmer in 1997. This, said Dr. Saunders, presages another active season. His study appeared in the May 15, 1997, issue of the journal *Geophysical Research Letters*.

The researchers suggest that warmer seas cause more water to evaporate from the surface. With evaporation, latent heat is released in the atmosphere, and the researchers believe that this is what imparts more energy to the embryonic storms coming out of Africa, making it more likely that they will develop into hurricanes. "It seems that this is a stronger effect that any other mechanism, like El Niño or the monsoon in the western Sahel," Dr. Saunders said.

The question, he said, is whether the rising sea temperature is a natural expression of the climate system's variability, independent of any influence from a warming atmosphere. Dr. Gray, for his part, says he believes the warmer ocean temperature is "a manifestation of a major change in North Atlantic ocean circulation." Stately currents in the North Atlantic undergo periodic shifts on decadal time scales. Dr. Gray said he believed that a new pattern was in place, and that it was likely to presage a decade or two of above-average hurricane activity.

"This is the greatest fear we have," he said, "that we're entering a new era. I believe we are."

If so, the federal study on hurricane damage may offer a preview of what lies ahead. In the study, Dr. Roger Pielke, Jr. of the National Center for Atmospheric Research in Boulder, Colorado, and Dr. Christopher Landsea of the National Oceanic and Atmospheric Administration's hurricane research division in Miami calculated how much damage would result from past hurricanes if they had occurred in 1995, when the coasts held many more people and much more wealth than earlier.

The calculation, which also accounts for inflation, shows that if the more numerous storms of the very active quarter century prior to 1970 were to hit the mainland now, each of the storms would cause far more damage than it did back then.

It has been suggested in the past that escalating hurricane damage in more recent decades has resulted from an increase in the number and severity of storms. The Pielke-Landsea analysis found this is not so. In fact, when all hurricane damage was assessed as if it had occurred in 1995, the four biggest hurricanes of the last eight years were no longer the most damaging in history. Andrew, which exacted an all-time record $26.5 billion in actual damages, was downgraded to second place by a monster that struck Florida and Alabama in 1926. Hugo (1989), Opal (1995) and Fran (1996) slip far down the list.

The analysis, its authors wrote, indicates clearly "that the United States has been fortunate in recent decades with regard to storm losses." Now, they wrote, multibillion-dollar losses may become increasingly frequent, and it may be "only a matter of time" before a single storm exacts $50 billion in damages.

—WILLIAM K. STEVENS, June 1997

4

CLIMATIC

CATASTROPHE

The worst of all natural disasters could come from a change in global climate. The world's climate has become several degrees warmer over the last century. Many climatologists now believe that the warming is not just the climate's natural variability but also in part the result of industrial activity.

If the warming trend continues, as seems likely, tens of millions of people who live in low-lying areas and oceanic islands may be forced out of their homes by rising waters by the end of the next century. And the number of people whose lives are disrupted by storm surges could double to 100 million.

If the warming trend is large enough, the Antarctic Ice Sheet could start to melt. This would cause a worldwide rise in sea level of 20 feet. The good news is that it would probably occur quite gradually, maybe over a period as long as 700 years.

Global warming would have profound biological effects. It would push northward the climatic belts in which crops like wheat could be grown. But it might also expand the world's equatorial deserts and, at worst, make the Tropics uninhabitable. In general, the world's weather is expected to become more violent as the average temperature rises.

If all these changes occur gradually, as is generally assumed to be likely, economies and ecosystems can probably adapt to them with varying degrees of success. A disturbing possibility, however, is that the world's climate might respond by suddenly switching from one state to another, an all-or-nothing response much as when a switch is flipped. Records of ancient climates suggest there have been dramatic fluctuations in global temperatures in the past.

If so, the world's biosystems evidently adapted even to those, but at a price that is hard to estimate. Whether biosystems today could adapt today to a sudden 10-degree temperature change is uncertain, especially as world agriculture now supports a large human population with perhaps not so large a margin of safety.

Coping with Climate Change;
If Climate Changes, Who Is Vulnerable?
Panels Offer Some Local Projections

IF MAINSTREAM SCIENTISTS ARE RIGHT in their forecast that the Earth will warm up substantially in the decades ahead, what will happen to a place like, say, New England? Will its brilliant fall foliage fade? Its sugar maples migrate to Canada? Its ski slopes turn to slush? Its tourists vanish?

As negotiators from around the world struggle to agree on cuts in emissions of heat-trapping greenhouse gases, scientists are trying to bring the issue of global warming and attendant changes in climate down out of the stratosphere of scientific debate and global diplomacy into the everyday world, where some local officials and citizens are starting to think more about how the predicted changes might affect them.

It is not an easy task. Experts find it difficult enough to predict how temperature and climate will change globally if industrial society continues to emit greenhouse gases like carbon dioxide. This is mainly because of imperfections in computer models of the atmosphere on which global predictions are based.

Forecasting the regional and local impact of climate change is even harder because the global models do not deal with climatic change on a regional and local scale very well. To make matters even more difficult, the global environment and human economy interact in complex and often unfathomable ways, creating environmental stresses that could be either worsened or mitigated by alterations in climate.

But nothing prevents scientists from zeroing in on areas and activities that could be vulnerable to the predicted alterations in climate, and they are doing so more intensively.

In the case of New England (and upstate New York), for instance, experts meeting at a federally sponsored workshop at the University of New Hampshire said that the predicted changes do indeed pose a substantial, though still potential, threat in coming decades to the region's forests, its winters, its trout fisheries and shoreline developments—many of the features, in fact, that together largely define the region's character. In some future autumn, the experts said, the landscape might be dominated not by the bright oranges, reds and yellows of maples, but by the duller brown of oaks and hickories that have migrated up from the South.

New England's very "sense of place" may be at risk, said Dr. Steven P. Hamburg, an ecologist at the University of Rhode Island.

But there will probably be gain as well as pain, winners as well as losers, and no country or region is likely to be affected in the same way. This point has been made again and again in the workshops held by the government's Global Change Research Program. The meetings are designed to produce a national assessment of the impact of climate change.

State and local officials, natural resource managers, businessmen and others who might have to deal with the effects of a changing climate have also been attending the meetings, watching and listening to scientists' slide presentations, and meeting in discussion groups, in the hallways and at the lunch table to exchange thoughts about what it all might mean.

In another forum, the Intergovernmental Panel on Climate Change, an international group of scientists that advises the climate negotiators under United Nations auspices, issued a report at a meeting in the Maldives identifying potential losses, gains and widely varying effects from climate change in different regions of the world.

On the negative side in North America, for instance, the panel found that forests and their wild inhabitants in the East and parts of the mountain West might not be able to migrate northward or upward fast enough or far enough to adjust to the warming climate. The group further concluded that water shortages in the southern plains could be made worse, that agriculture in the Southeast and southern plains could be at risk, that deaths from extreme heat in Northern cities could increase and that coastal development could be threatened by rising seas.

On the positive side, the panel found that, for example, agriculture in the Northern United States and southern Canada, on the West Coast and in parts of the interior West could benefit, as could the magnificent ever-green forests of the West Coast; that milder winters could cut the number of cold-weather deaths and the cost of heating and snow clearance; and that northern waters could be open for navigation longer. In fact, the re-port said, the Arctic Ocean might become ice-free, opening a new trade route between Europe and Asia.

American society might be able to cope relatively easily with any sin-gle effect of climate change, said Dr. David S. Shriner, an ecologist at the Oak Ridge National Laboratory in Tennessee who was a lead author of the North American chapter of the intergovernmental panel's report. But he said that because there were likely to be several effects, all occurring at the same time, they would pose "increasing challenges" for policymakers, re-source managers and citizens, especially because any changes would be difficult to predict.

One measure of the difficulty is that the intergovernmental panel's forecast of global warming specifies a wide range of possible increases in average surface temperature over the next century, from 2 to 6 degrees Fahrenheit; the panel's best estimate is about 3.5 degrees if greenhouse gas emissions are not reduced. Moreover, while the Earth's surface has warmed by about 1 degree over the last century, scientists are not sure how much of that is natural and how much has been caused by greenhouse emissions.

Still, there are some early signs of actual climate change, and in some respects they appear in line with experts' admittedly very general notions of what is vulnerable and what is not. A case in point is Alaska, where, sci-entists at the University of Alaska said, the average warm-season tempera-ture at Fairbanks has risen by nearly 3 degrees Fahrenheit in the last half century. While the temperature reached 80 degrees for about a week in the early 1950s, it now does so for nearly three weeks. These figures were typ-ical for central Alaska and much of the western North American Arctic, the scientists said.

It is possible that this warming could be an expression of the climate system's natural variability. But it is just the kind of temperature change the intergovernmental panel predicted; the Arctic is expected to warm more than the global average (while the Tropics are expected to warm less).

Alaska is already experiencing the low range of the warming the panel predicted for the globe as a whole by the year 2100, Dr. Glenn P. Juday, a forest ecologist at the university in Fairbanks, said at the New England workshop. While only time will tell whether the Alaskan warm-up has been caused by greenhouse gases, he said, "the kinds of change you might expect from global warming are happening" in the state right now.

The evidence of Alaskan climate change is substantial, the scientists said: Glaciers have generally receded and typically become about 30 feet thinner in the last 40 years. There is about 5 percent less sea ice in the Bering Sea now than in the 1950s. Permafrost is thawing, and as it does, the ground is subsiding and holes are opening in roads. The thawing has also led to landslides and erosion, threatening roads and bridges and causing local floods.

Traditional ice cellars in northern villages have thawed and become useless. Melting sea ice has made hunting more dangerous for native people. More precipitation falls as rain than snow. But where it remains cold enough to snow, annual snowfall has increased, as would be expected in a generally warmer and therefore moister global atmosphere. The snow also melts faster, at least at low altitudes, and the intergovernmental panel forecasts more running and standing water.

The state's vast evergreen forests, called taiga, are under climatic siege, and Dr. Juday said their growth rate has gone "into the tank," in lockstep with the temperature rise.

The new report of the intergovernmental panel said that tundra and taiga in North America may be reduced by two thirds in the next century and that the southern boundary of the area covered by permafrost should shift northward by about 300 miles over the next 50 years, threatening roads, buildings, pipelines and other structures.

But there is good news for the Arctic, too, and there may be more if the warming is a long-term one. With less snow and more rain in coastal areas, for instance, there are fewer avalanches. The growing season is longer, and the intergovernmental panel says that some of the Arctic may eventually open up to farming. Less ice offshore could aid oil and gas production, and warmer water could help fisheries. Heating costs could fall. Tourists could have easier access to the region. Once the permafrost is finished melting, construction should be easier than before.

The Arctic is among the regions most vulnerable to climate change, according to the panel's report. Other highly vulnerable places, it said, include small islands, many of which could be all but inundated by rising seas caused by heat-induced expansion of ocean water and melting ice sheets. The report specifically cited the Bahamas, the Maldives and the Pacific states of Kiribati and the Marshall Islands as examples of the most threatened spots. It said that as much as 80 percent of the Marshalls' territory could be drowned by a one-meter, or 3.28-foot, rise in sea level, which is in the high end of the range predicted by the panel by 2100. (The best estimate is a rise of about a foot and a half by then, with a continuing rise after that.)

Some 70 million people in low-lying areas of Bangladesh could be displaced by a one-meter rise, the panel said. Such a rise would also threaten the coastal zone on which Tokyo, Osaka and Nagoya sit in Japan, not to mention China and the Atlantic and Gulf Coasts of the United States, according to the panel, and salt water could intrude on inland rivers, threatening some supplies of fresh water.

The opposite problem, too little water, could be worsened in arid areas like the Middle East and parts of Africa, according to the intergovernmental panel. Global warming is expected to make droughts more frequent and severe in areas prone to them. Largely for this reason, according to the panel, Africa may be the continent most vulnerable to climate change, because its economy consists largely of rain-fed agriculture and many of its farmers are too poor and ill equipped to adapt.

Australia and parts of Latin America, too, were judged vulnerable to drought, and the panel projected falling agricultural production for some major crops in Mexico, Central America and parts of South America.

On the other hand, increased rainfall in temperate zones, combined with a warmer climate, longer growing seasons and the fertilizing properties of atmospheric carbon dioxide, might spur agriculture there. Much of the increase in precipitation is expected to come not from the steady, gentle rains favored by farmers, however, but from heavy storms that could increase flooding. Evidence of an increase in these heavy storms has already been detected in North America. Northern Europe, according to the panel, may be hit by more floods, while southern Europe is more vulnerable to drought.

In southern Asia, where hundreds of millions of rural dwellers depend on the seasonal flow of water from melting snow and ice in the Himalayas, there might be more water in the short term but less in the long run as glaciers and snow cover shrink.

As many of these examples suggest, much of the potential impact of climate change has to do with changes in the distribution of water around the world; that is, the planetary hydrological cycle involving evaporation of water from the Earth's surface, precipitation, freezing and melting. In North America, for instance, water is the common factor tying together many impacts across many regions, the intergovernmental panel found. A warmer climate is expected to affect not only the kinds of weather people experience—more severe rainstorms and also more severe droughts—but also the availability of water in many regions. Some are likely to get more, others less.

Climate change may have serious repercussions for human health, said the intergovernmental panel. The ranges of mosquitoborne tropical diseases like malaria, dengue fever, and encephalitis, and waterborne diarrheal diseases could expand, for instance. And in a more direct effect, heat-related summertime deaths are expected to increase in northern American and European cities, and cold-related deaths to decrease.

The intergovernmental report said the expected net effect on total deaths is unclear in Europe, but a leading American expert on the subject said that in this country, the increase in heat deaths was likely to outweigh the reduction in deaths from cold. The reason, said Dr. Laurence S. Kalkstein of the University of Delaware, is that many cold-season deaths are related to diseases like flu, which are transmitted in closely confined winter quarters. Climate change is not likely to alter that picture of confinement very much in Northern cities, he said.

On the other hand, he told another recent federal workshop at Pennsylvania State University, summertime heat deaths in Northern cities are almost certain to rise substantially if the climate warms as predicted. First, he said, Northerners are not as acclimatized to heat as Southerners are. Second, Northern buildings, especially in crowded cities, are not constructed to promote cooling. Even air-conditioning is no automatic fix, he said, because many inner-city dwellers cannot afford it. "There is no doubt in my mind that we have a problem," he said.

—WILLIAM K. STEVENS, September 1997

Warmer, Wetter, Sicker: Linking Climate to Health

SCIENTISTS HAVE long theorized that climatic changes related to global warming could unleash outbreaks of diseases like malaria, dengue fever, cholera and heatstroke. But with the modest amount of warming experienced so far, they have been unable to produce much hard evidence.

Now the experts have a research gift from an unlikely benefactor: El Niño. Combined with an underlying global warming trend, say scientists who track such things, El Niño will probably make 1998 unusually warm, possibly the warmest year in several centuries. And the heavy rains, droughts and other extreme weather fostered by El Niño over the last year are precisely what many scientists expect will also result from a predicted warming of the globe in the decades ahead.

So, in the belief that 1997 and 1998 would provide a taste of what is to come, those who pay attention to the health effects of climate are now pulling together data about weather-related illness and death. Though most of the evidence is circumstantial, consisting of correlations and coincidences, it suggests that amid all the scientific smoke there is some fire.

These are some of the clues:

- The World Health Organization reports "quantitative leaps" in the incidence of malaria around the world, coincident with extreme weather events associated with El Niño. Heat and variations in rainfall affect transmission of the disease by mosquitoes.
- Tens of thousands of people in Kenya and Somalia were afflicted by another mosquitoborne disease, Rift Valley fever, and at least 200 died, after the heaviest rains since 1961, attributed to El Niño, fell on the region.

- The incidence of cholera increased markedly in 1998 in Latin America, where an epidemic had already been in progress for seven years, and parts of Africa. In both cases the surge in cases was associated with heavy rainfall and floods linked to El Niño.

- In the southern Rockies, a warm, wet winter brought on by El Niño produced abundant food and cover for deer mice, which transmit the deadly hantavirus to humans. The number of mice has increased, and the deaths of three people have been ascribed to the disease. Federal disease-control agents are still analyzing the problem.

- Forest fires in Southeast Asia, made possible by a killing drought attributed to El Niño, subjected hundreds of thousands of people to respiratory ailments.

While this and similar evidence is sifted and tested, scientists are also beginning to focus more closely on the health impact of extreme weather events quite apart from El Niño, especially in the United States. One thing they are finding is that there is a statistically significant association in the United States between heavy rainstorms and outbreaks of waterborne diseases. These include hepatitis, *E. coli* infections and the cryptosporidium parasite that infected 400,000 people and killed 50 to 100 in Milwaukee in 1993, as well as other gastrointestinal diseases caused by viruses, bacteria and parasites.

If the relationship between heavy rain and disease is a solid one and climate experts are right, the country may be in for a surge of climatically induced waterborne illness.

Analyses of the last century's weather records by the National Climatic Data Center have found that extremely heavy rainstorms have become more common. For example, single rainfalls on the order of eight and nine inches each deluged the Boston area in mid-June, the Ohio Valley in late June and south-central Tennessee in mid-July of 1998.

Climatologists say that this is just the kind of increase in extreme rainstorms that would be expected in a warming atmosphere, which holds more moisture and causes more water to evaporate from the oceans. The heavier rain that results is more likely to cause floods that not only kill people but also overwhelm drinking-water purification systems.

"If extreme weather events are part of a changing climate," said Dr. Paul R. Epstein, associate director of the Center for Health and the Global Environment at Harvard Medical School, "we've seen lots of evidence of the profound health effects associated with climate change." East Africa, he said, especially illustrates the risk to health posed by climatic factors. There, simultaneous outbreaks of cholera, malaria and Rift Valley fever followed heavy rains and flooding.

Dr. Epstein has long held the view that global warming will have a serious effect on health. His group at Harvard has also made a compilation of possible health effects of El Niño 1997.

The view has provoked argument. In the always contentious debate over climate change and the uncertainties that attend it, it has been especially difficult to get a handle on the question of health and disease. The Intergovernmental Panel on Climate Change, an international group of scientists advising the United Nations, recognized this in its most recent report, issued in 1995.

The panel predicted that if emissions of heat-trapping industrial waste gases like carbon dioxide were not reduced, the average surface temperature of the Earth would rise by about 3.5 degrees Fahrenheit by the end of the next century. This is roughly half the amount of warming experienced since the depths of the last ice age. About a degree of warming has taken place in the last century, and the latest surface readings combined with tree-ring studies made by climatologists at the University of East Anglia in Britain indicate that 1997 was the warmest year in the last 1,000.

Some recent events, the intergovernmental panel said in 1995, might plausibly be early signals of climate-induced changes in human health. The panel cited a surge in heat-related deaths in India in 1995 (there was a similar surge in 1998), changes in the ranges of some insectborne diseases and the spread of cholera along coastal areas in some developing countries.

But the group also said it was "not possible to attribute particular, isolated events to a change in climate or weather pattern."

The problem, said Dr. Duane Gubler, director of the division of vectorborne infectious diseases at the federal Centers for Disease Control and Prevention in Atlanta, "is that we may see some correlations" between climate and disease outbreaks, "but we don't know whether it's cause and effect." So, he said, "we're kind of cautious" in tying climatic change to changes in health.

Not a few experts point out, for instance, that while a warming atmosphere would theoretically be expected to expand the range of mosquito-borne tropical diseases like malaria and dengue fever, reality is not so simple.

Temperature, humidity, rainfall and other weather factors are indeed some of the main things that influence transmission of the diseases. In some instances, temperature increases the virulence of the disease itself, by prompting viruses to multiply more. Heavier rainfall creates more standing water for some kinds of mosquitoes to breed in, and populations soar. Drought encourages people to store water in open containers, with the same result.

But in the developed countries, experts like Dr. Gubler say, public-health pluses like pest control and better living conditions (more tightly built houses, for example) have pretty much slammed the door on epidemics of mosquitoborne illness. Until early this century, malaria, dengue fever and yellow fever were common in the United States. Today, outbreaks of those diseases are small, isolated and rare. Usually, says Dr. Gubler, the cases have arrived from somewhere else.

This public-health success, a number of experts say, would probably stop any climate-induced invasion by mosquitoborne diseases at the United States border—as indeed might have happened already: dengue fever, resurgent in the Caribbean and Central America in recent years, has not become a major problem in the United States, even though, Dr. Gubler says, the temperature along the Gulf Coast is higher than in the Caribbean. While Texas reported only a handful of cases in 1995 and again in 1997, said Dr. Gubler, there were thousands of cases a stone's throw away, in Mexico.

Dr. Gubler, Dr. Epstein and many others agree that developing countries, with less effective and in some cases nonexistent controls on mosquitoes, would be highly vulnerable to any climatically induced surge in diseases borne by vectors, or animals, usually insects, that carry a disease from a host to another animal.

They also agree that efforts to improve public-health measures there and limit climatic change globally are necessary.

But the richer countries, including the United States, may not be immune to climate-sensitive health problems. Two big cases in point are heat waves and waterborne diseases.

Many climate experts say that heat waves are likely to become more frequent and intense, and therefore more deadly. If they are right, what happened in Texas may be a foretaste. More than 100 people died there in a heat wave that saw temperatures in Dallas rise above 100 degrees Fahrenheit for weeks on end. It was even worse in India, where the most intense heat wave in 50 years sent the temperature soaring above 120 degrees in some places. Nearly 1,300 people died.

Skeptics point out that people in the southern United States have become acclimatized to heat, and argue that Northerners will adapt if the climate warms. But Dr. Laurence S. Kalkstein of the University of Delaware, who has long studied the subject, says that people become vulnerable to heat whenever it reaches a certain threshold above what they are used to— even if they are used to high temperatures. The lethal Southern and Indian heat waves in 1998 may provide some evidence of this.

The important unanswered question, Dr. Kalkstein said, is whether heat waves will get hotter with the general climate. "If New York's climate becomes more like Jacksonville's and all the days stay about the same in the summer," he said, "I think New Yorkers will acclimatize." But if hotter heat waves are then superimposed on top of a generally warmer climate, "we are going to get more deaths," he said.

Skeptics also point out that cold-related deaths would probably drop in the winter. But Dr. Kalkstein believes that heat-related deaths will more than offset this. Many cold-season deaths, he explains, result from diseases like flu that are transmitted in confined spaces in buttoned-up winter buildings.

Climate change is not likely to alter this picture much, Dr. Kalkstein says.

Experts are just beginning to get a firm handle on weather-related outbreaks of waterborne disease in the United States.

One problem is that heavy rainfalls tend to overwhelm sewage-treatment systems early in a flood, catching those who operate the systems unprepared. As a result, disease organisms "ride the initial wave that comes downstream," in the first hour or two of a storm, infecting people before anything can be done, said Dr. Dennis Juranek, the associate director of the division of parasitic diseases at the Centers for Disease Control and Prevention.

The difficulty is compounded by the fact that outbreaks of diarrheal diseases, the most common waterborne maladies, are not usually perceived as a public-health emergency—even though they are sometimes fatal to people whose immune systems are depressed—and therefore are probably underreported.

Diarrheal diseases do not "cause people to fall over or bleed out of the eyes or mouth," Dr. Juranek said, adding, "It has to be something big like Milwaukee" to gain attention. Even in Milwaukee, "we came within a hair's width" of failing to find out that the cryptosporidium outbreak of 1993 was waterborne.

Scientists at the University of South Florida, the University of Maryland and the National Climatic Data Center are taking some of the first steps in pinning down the cause and effect between climate and disease. They have plotted more than 300 outbreaks of waterborne disease over the last 50 years against the distribution of heavy rains.

Although the data are still being analyzed, "we can demonstrate increased probability of waterborne outbreaks when there are extreme events," said Dr. Joan Rose, a microbiologist at the University of South Florida.

In 1982 to 1983, the last big El Niño period before 1997 to 1998, 60 to 70 percent of the outbreaks were associated with extreme rainfalls, she said.

—WILLIAM K. STEVENS, August 1998

Dead Trees and Shriveling Glaciers as Alaska Melts

MIGHTY AND MAJESTIC, THE RIVER of ice snakes down to Prince William Sound between classically craggy mountains wreathed in clouds. Through the mist-streaked windows of a light plane, Columbia Glacier's huge mass and aquamarine-flecked desolation have an almost visceral impact.

But like much of the rest of Alaska, the glacier is not what it used to be.

Not so long ago, cruise ships nosed right up to the glacier's 200-foot-high front wall to watch icebergs break off and crash into the sound. That is impossible today. The front has retreated by more than eight miles in the last 16 years, and ships are separated from it by a vast expanse of melting icebergs, penned in by a rocky shoal that stretches from where the shrinking glacier's front wall used to be to where it is now.

Alaska is thawing, and much of northern Russia and Canada with it, and many scientists say that the warming of these cold regions is one of the most telling signals that the planet's climate is changing. Experts have long said that in an era of global warming, this bellwether region should warm more and faster than the Earth as a whole, and that is just how things are turning out.

The signs are everywhere.

Scientists employing laser instruments have confirmed that many of Alaska's hundreds of glaciers are retreating. The warmer atmosphere, which holds more moisture, has produced more snow to feed the glaciers, but longer, warmer summers have in many cases melted them even faster than the heavier snows can build them up. Late summer, countless streams run full and chalky with tiny rock particles pulverized to dust by the glaciers.

The region's permafrost, ground that is perpetually frozen, is thawing in Alaska's interior, and pockets of underground ice trapped in the frost are

103

melting with it. Over thousands of miles, big patches of forest are drowning and turning gray as the ground sinks under them and swamp water floods them. Here and there, deep holes have opened in the Earth. Here and there, roadside utility poles destabilized by the melting tilt at crazy angles. So do trees, creating a phenomenon known as drunken forest.

The intermittent character of the land's settling—the permafrost comes in patches in most of the state, and not every patch has ice pockets—wreaks havoc on paved roads. Between here and Fairbanks, 360 miles away, many stretches of highway are like ocean waves, and driving on them often requires vigilance. Maintenance crews in the summer are constantly busy not just repairing irregular breaks and cracks in roads, but constantly re-repairing them, at substantial cost.

Along the Fairbanks-to-Valdez stretch, entire mountainsides of spruce forest, prime timberland that used to be part of the magnificent taiga, the vast boreal forest of conifers that rings the world's northern latitudes, are dead and gray. The trees have been weakened by climate-related stress, then killed by spruce bark beetles whose population, scientists say, has exploded in the higher temperatures. "It has moved into high gear in the last six or seven years," said Dr. Glenn P. Juday, a forest ecologist at the University of Alaska. "It's just rolling through the forest."

About the magnitude of the warming, there is little doubt. While the average surface temperature of the globe has risen over the last century by 1 degree Fahrenheit or a little more, it has increased over the last 30 years by up to about 5 degrees in Alaska, Siberia and northwestern Canada, say scientists at the University of Alaska and elsewhere. The warming has been most pronounced in winter.

Scientists are not certain how much of the regional warming relates to overall warming of the globe, if any. Some of it, they say, is clearly the result of a change in prevailing patterns of atmospheric circulation, beginning in the mid-1970s, which generally redirected the flow of warm air from the Pacific toward Alaska. But experts on climate change, like Dr. Gunter Weller of the University of Alaska in Fairbanks, point out that big areas of northern Russia not affected by the circulation change have warmed as much as Alaska. Moreover, say other experts, it is possible that global warming had something to do with the shift in circulation.

A number of experts believe the regional thaw has resulted from a combination of natural and human-induced climate change. Mainstream scientists predict that globally, the average surface temperature will rise by 2 to 6 degrees Fahrenheit over the next century, with a best estimate of about 3.5 degrees, if emissions of heat-trapping industrial waste gases like carbon dioxide are not reduced. The gases are produced by burning fossil fuels like coal, oil and natural gas.

The scientists say that Alaska and other far northern continental regions should warm about twice as much as the average for the globe. Two main reasons lie behind this: as ice and snow melt, less heat is reflected off the land, amplifying the warming. And at these latitudes, the atmosphere is more stable in winter and spring. This confines more heat to its lower layers.

Whatever the combination of causes of Alaska's warming, the catalogue of effects is substantial.

Thirty years ago, the temperature at Fairbanks reached 80 degrees for only about a week in the summer. Now it hits or exceeds that mark for a total of about three weeks. On average, Dr. Juday says, a summer day is about 11 percent warmer than it was three decades ago.

When Dr. Weller moved to Fairbanks 30 years ago, winter temperatures frequently dipped well below minus 40. In the last two decades, the number of sub-40-degree days has dropped substantially compared with the three preceding decades.

In the Bering Sea, scientists have found, the extent of sea ice has decreased by about 5 percent over the last 30 years. In Nanana, inland near Fairbanks, people since 1917 have taken great pains to measure the exact moment when the Tanana River ice breaks up each spring. A lucrative lottery depends on the result. Four of the earliest breakups in that 81-year span have been in the 1990s.

In the interior, higher temperatures have been accompanied by more snow in the winter (as is well known, extreme cold means a drier atmosphere and less precipitation), but also less rain in the summer. For Alaska agriculture, which is already limited by a scarcity of suitable land, the warming has been a double-edged sword. The good news is that the growing season is about 20 percent longer; the bad news is that sufficient water for crops is often lacking.

"It's changed dramatically since the eighties," said Scott Miller, who farms a big, flat spread of barley, oats and hay about a two-hour drive south of Fairbanks, within sight of the snow-capped Alaska Range. There, with a brilliant sun beating down and the temperature heading toward 80 on a recent summer day, Mr. Miller explained that in the 1980s, it rained practically all summer, and there was a danger of frost in July. "Now," he said, "we're way on the other end of the spectrum; we're usually hurting for water, and there's more heat."

On the other hand, according to the 1997 study, longer summers have allowed the state's vibrant tourist industry to expand. Other long-

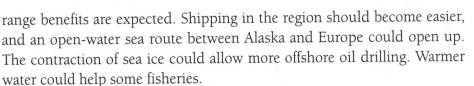

range benefits are expected. Shipping in the region should become easier, and an open-water sea route between Alaska and Europe could open up. The contraction of sea ice could allow more offshore oil drilling. Warmer water could help some fisheries.

But at the moment, the warming is perhaps most evident in its effects on forests, permafrost and glaciers.

On a clear morning a few miles southwest of Fairbanks, from where the gleaming white pyramid of Mount McKinley rose hazily in the distance, Dr. Juday knelt on the floor of the Bonanza Creek Experimental Forest, a long-term ecological research reservation. A vintage old-growth forest of white spruce not far from the Arctic Circle, it is in the middle of the taiga. Moss-covered logs litter the ground. The spruces themselves, their short, needled branches draped with feathery lichens much like Spanish moss, tower overhead, straight and tall, rising to 100 feet.

"We're talking about the cream of the crop—the very best forests we have in interior Alaska," Dr. Juday said. As he spoke, he set up a handheld global positioning instrument and contacted overhead satellites to fix the spot's coordinates. The purpose was to aid airborne scientists who later would survey the forest for climate-related damage—in this case, the extent to which the crowns of the big spruces have been snapped off by heavy snows.

Normally, the snows at that latitude are light and fluffy. But recently they have become heavier, apparently a result of the changing climate. The weight of two especially heavy snowfalls in the late 1980s and early 1990s broke off the tops of trees. "There was an incredible outbreak of insects following that," and they attacked the trees, Dr. Juday said as he pointed out two topless spruce giants.

On top of that, he said, the warming climate, coupled with less summer precipitation, has stunted trees' growth. The crowns of aspens, for instance, look puny, and that is where the recent growth would have taken place. Besides promoting a bigger buildup of tree-eating insects, the warming has prompted some species, like the spruce budworm, to move farther north.

"These trees are in real trouble," Dr. Juday said. "We've got a sick forest here."

Farther south, much of the forest is more than sick; it is dead or dying. In a broad swath stretching 300 or 400 miles along the state's southern tier, from the Kenai Peninsula south of Anchorage past the spectacular Chugach Mountains north and northeast of here, chunks of landscape have turned red (freshly killed) or gray (long dead). Spruce bark beetles are the killers, and they are "basically eliminating the forest canopy," said Jerry Boughton, who heads the United States Forest Service's regional forest health program, based in Anchorage. A third to half of Alaska's white spruce have died in the last 15 years.

Several factors have combined to produce this ecological holocaust, said Mr. Boughton, not least the fact that the forest is older, and therefore more vulnerable to insect attack. "But certainly, the warming has created a better environment for the bark beetle to expand," he said. In fact, mainstream scientists say, that is how the predicted global warming will often make itself felt: by exacerbating stresses of many kinds.

Many experts expect the taiga to migrate slowly north, replacing treeless tundra, if the warming continues or intensifies. In other regions of the world, other species from farther south would normally move in behind them. But in Alaska, which is bounded on the south by ocean, it is unclear what will happen.

"I don't know of any trees in the Gulf of Alaska," Dr. Juday said.

Dr. Vladimir E. Romanovsky, formerly of Moscow State University but now of the University of Alaska, has seen lots of permafrost; it is his area of expertise. But if he wants to see firsthand what can happen when permafrost melts, he need look no farther than the field next to his mother-in-law's home outside Fairbanks. There, a hole 15 feet long, six feet across and eight feet deep has recently opened in the ground.

The hole, with doomed saplings and sod lying in the bottom, is a thermokarst: a sinking plot of ground caused by thawing permafrost. Growing numbers of thermokarsts now abound in Alaska.

Construction has long been known to thaw permafrost if not undertaken with care, but now something different is happening. A thicker layer of insulating snow in the winter, combined with warmer summer weather, is causing undisturbed permafrost to thaw, creating an uneven and sometimes crater-pocked landscape.

Thawing permafrost has forced the relocation roads and runways. Agricultural fields have been damaged and houses have tilted off kilter. Roads and bridges have been abandoned, as has a hospital in the town of

Kotzebue. Even the site for the university's building for international arctic research, under construction in Fairbanks, had to be moved.

Along interior roads, drivers can see the telltale sign of sinking ground: a stand of larch, its branches looking delicate and spidery, but gray rather than green, standing in the water of a stretch of muskeg, or subarctic swamp. When a thermokarst develops, the swampy water fills it, and the trees die.

Dr. Romanovsky said measurements from boreholes drilled into the ground show many areas are mere tenths of a degree from the melting point and will thaw if the warming continues. If the warming runs its course as predicted, thermokarsting will eventually be complete, the permafrost line will have moved farther north (it has already migrated 80 miles in the last century in some places), and a new stability will have set in, making construction and maintenance easier than before the thaw. The transition is the problem.

When the Columbia Glacier was first studied a century ago, it was advancing rapidly from the land into Prince William Sound. The advance stopped about 1923 and was followed by a slight pullback. More recently the glacier was stable, its leading edge anchored to a broad underwater shoal of rocky debris, called a moraine, that the glacier had pushed ahead of it as it advanced. Each summer the glacier would fall back a bit, but would advance in the winter and reattach itself to the moraine.

Then, in 1983, it failed to reattach, and the retreat was on. It has been retreating toward the shore at an average rate of half a mile a year since. The moraine pens up the eight-mile field of icebergs that holds ships away from the glacier's front.

What touched off the pell-mell pullback? "My belief is that it is climate," said Dr. Will Harrison, a geophysicist at the University of Alaska, who is an expert on glaciers. One theory is that the warmer environment prevented the glacier from reattaching itself to the moraine after the seasonal summer fallback. "Once climate kicks it off, you can't stop it," Dr. Harrison said of the retreat. "Once the bullet's fired, that's it." Many climate experts believe that in general, abrupt changes like this, rather than gradual ones, will typify a warming climate.

Alaska has more than 1,000 glaciers, big and small, and together they make up the fourth-largest collection of ice in the world, after Antarctica,

Greenland and the neighboring Queen Elizabeth Islands of the high Arctic. And as is true of mountain glaciers generally, many of Alaska's are retreating, ever faster in recent years.

Recent mapping of a sampling of nine glaciers, said Dr. Harrison, has revealed that all have thinned substantially at lower elevations, probably because of increased melting in the summer. But at higher elevations, most of the glaciers have thickened, probably because of increased winter precipitation. Still, in most instances, the melting at the base of the glaciers has outstripped the new ice provided by winter snows, and the trend has been especially pronounced in the last five years. "Something's happened here," Dr. Harrison said.

Indeed.

Given the uncertainty of climate predictions, the future is unclear. "But each year and each month that the temperature doesn't drop down," said Dr. Juday, "is confirmation that the whole system has been kicked up" to a new climatic state.

—WILLIAM K. STEVENS, August 1998

If Climate Changes, It May Change Quickly

IN THE DEBATE OVER GLOBAL warming, there has been a widespread assumption that if humans are changing the Earth's climate, the effects will be felt gradually and smoothly, making it easier to adapt to the change.

But a growing accumulation of geological evidence is making it ever clearer that in the past, the climate has undergone drastic changes in temperature and rainfall patterns in the space of a human lifetime, in a decade or in even less time.

The implications for federal and international climate policy are enormous because heat-trapping carbon dioxide produced by the burning of fossil fuels like coal and oil is steadily accumulating in the atmosphere and putting increasing pressure on the climate system.

Many experts believe that late in the next century, concentrations of the gas will be double their preindustrial levels. If that happens, mainstream scientists say, the average surface temperature of the globe will rise by 2 to 6 degrees Fahrenheit, compared with a rise of 5 to 9 degrees since the depths of the last ice age. That much warming, the scientists say, would lead to rising seas and more severe droughts, rainstorms, heat waves and floods, as well as broad shifts in climatic and agricultural zones that would benefit some regions and harm others.

Could the pressure exerted on the climate system by carbon dioxide and other greenhouse gases trip a trigger at some point, forcing these changes on humanity suddenly rather than gradually?

Scientists do not know for sure, but the question gives them pause.

"The climate system is an angry beast and we are poking it with sticks," said Dr. Wallace S. Broecker of Columbia University's Lamont-Doherty Earth Observatory, who was one of the first to raise the alarm about abrupt climate change. "We don't know whether it's going to pay attention to the pokes. But if it does, it might rise up and do something we don't like."

In uncovering one of the latest pieces of evidence of abrupt climate change, American scientists led by Dr. Jeffrey P. Severinghaus of the University of Rhode Island examined climatic clues taken from corings of ancient ice in Greenland.

The Severinghaus team determined that when the world began its final ascent out of the last ice age more than 11,000 years ago, temperatures in Greenland initially spiked upward by about 9 to 18 degrees Fahrenheit—at least a third, and perhaps more, of the total recovery to today's warmth—in, at most, mere decades and probably less than a single decade. They also found that the impact of the sudden warming had been felt at least throughout the Northern Hemisphere.

That amount of heating, coming so quickly, is astounding, said Dr. Richard Alley of Pennsylvania State University, a member of the study team. Another recent study, by Dr. Peter deMenocal, a paleoclimatologist at Lamont-Doherty, examined clues in Atlantic Ocean sediments off subtropical North Africa. He discovered that every 1,500 years or so since the end of the ice age, ocean temperatures there have fluctuated widely and abruptly.

In a cold phase, they fell by 5 to 15 degrees, and seasonal rains on the continent were severely curtailed—all within no more than 50 to 100 years, and possibly less (the sediment analysis is not fine enough to tell). Then, in another 1,500 years, the picture reversed just as abruptly, causing flooding rains and creating widespread lakes in what is now the Sahara.

"The transitions are sharp," Dr. deMenocal said. "Climate changes that we thought should take thousands of years to happen occur within a generation or two" at most. The changes may have wreaked havoc on nascent civilizations in Africa and the Middle East. "It was certainly something that would have rocked somebody's world," Dr. deMenocal said.

Until recently, scientists thought that the climate system responded to what they call "forcings"—like, for instance, rising atmospheric concentrations of carbon dioxide or stronger solar radiation—much as a stereo set does: turn up the volume and the sound gets gradually louder. But now it is increasingly evident that the system behaves, at least some of the time, more like an electrical switch: increasing pressure has no effect (or a relatively small effect, in the case of climate) until a certain threshold is reached, and then the switch clicks, initiating a new state.

Dr. Kendrick Taylor, a paleoclimatologist at the Desert Research Institute of Nevada at Reno, a division of the University of Nevada, says there is "a growing awareness" that the question of climatic thresholds is serious. Dr. Taylor, like Dr. Severinghaus, has also found that the warming in Greenland at the end of the ice age was abrupt.

"If we find out that we're far away from one of these thresholds, we might be able to change atmospheric carbon dioxide a lot and not have any impact," Dr. Taylor said. "On the other hand, we may find we're very close to one of these thresholds and that as a society it may behoove us to pay more attention."

There are other uncertainties as well. For one thing, no one knows at what point in the future the climate switch might be tripped, naturally or otherwise, or where various thresholds might lie. It is "like walking the plank blindfolded," said Dr. Thomas J. Crowley, a paleoclimatologist at Texas A&M University in College Station.

It is also unclear to what extent the big, abrupt climatic shifts in Greenland affected the rest of the world. Changes in global temperature tend to be more extreme at high latitudes like Greenland than they are farther south, and the biggest jumps could have been limited to the North Atlantic region.

But the idea that thresholds exist is becoming widely accepted, and the suspicion that they may be the dominant mode of climatic change is growing.

The question surged to prominence in 1993, when scientists reported on the basis of Greenland ice corings that the climate of the last interglacial period, a 10,000-year warm period that began about 130,000 years ago and at some times was slightly warmer than today, fluctuated widely from warmth to extreme cold in spans of decades or less.

Another Greenland coring, however, suggested that the climate of this long-ago interglacial interval, called the Eemian period, had been in a stable state of warmth. Scientists said the first ice sample had apparently been distorted when the bottom of the flowing glacier from which it was taken passed over uneven ground.

But ice core studies in the last five years have avoided that problem by focusing on more recent strata within the ice, most notably those representing the climate in and around a centuries-long period, called the Younger Dryas, that began about 12,000 years ago. The Younger Dryas was the last gasp of the last ice age, a relatively brief plunge back into glacial cold after the climate had already warmed up.

In 1993, a team headed by Dr. Alley found that the accumulation of snow in Greenland had doubled sharply, in possibly one to three years, as the Younger Dryas gave way to warmer temperatures. In sub-Arctic latitudes like Greenland, more snow and ice accumulate in warm periods, when there is more moisture in the atmosphere, than in cold ones.

Recently, a team headed by Dr. Taylor reported that it had analyzed another Greenland core segment and discovered that most of the transition from the deep freeze of the Younger Dryas to the warmth of the last 10,000 years, called the Holocene period, had come in two quick temperature jumps, each of nearly 10 degrees and each lasting less than a decade, within a 40-year transition period.

Dr. Severinghaus and his colleagues have made a similar discovery and, in addition, have found evidence that the climatic change signified by the ice corings extended beyond Greenland to the wider world. The discoveries were reported in the journal *Nature*.

Scientists have a number of ways to detect climatic changes preserved in ancient ice. They can analyze bubbles in the ice for the presence of lighter or heavier forms, or isotopes, of oxygen; the changing ratios of the two forms allow researchers to infer temperature change. They can analyze the dust content of the cores to infer cold periods (colder is drier) and warm ones (warmer is wetter).

Dr. Severinghaus used yet another technique, one especially suited to detecting abrupt change. The technique analyzes the behavior of relatively lighter and heavier isotopes of nitrogen.

In a stratum of ice representing a time period when the temperature changed sharply, the lighter forms migrate to the top while heavier ones gravitate to the bottom. Applying this analysis to the Younger Dryas-Holocene transition, the Severinghaus team discovered that the transition had begun with a sharp rise of about 9 to 18 degrees Fahrenheit, on the way to an increase of about 27 degrees. A computer analysis of the nitrogen isotopes' behavior suggested that the initial jump had taken place in less than a decade.

The team also looked for methane, which in cold times is locked up in frozen wetlands but in warm ones is liberated into the atmosphere as the wetlands thaw. The ice core record showed that within no more than 30 years after the initial spike of warming that ended the Younger Dryas, atmospheric methane had increased. Because the thawing wetlands were presumably far from the permanently frozen Greenland ice cap, the scientists inferred that the climatic change after the Younger Dryas had extended at least through the Northern Hemisphere.

The methane results say nothing, however, about how large the abrupt temperature change was in lower latitudes, away from Greenland. Since the average global temperature of the world is now 5 to 9 degrees higher than in the ice age, compared with the 27-degree rise detected in Greenland, it suggests that the impact of the sudden initial warming following the Younger Dryas was somewhat more muted in what is now the United States than in the sub-Arctic. Dr. Crowley said computer simulations suggested that the size of the temperature changes in the Northeastern United States might be about 20 percent of those in Greenland. In the case of the rebound from the Younger Dryas's chill, that would be about 2 to 3.5 degrees.

But even modest changes can have big effects. The sulfuric haze cast aloft by the 1991 eruption of the Mount Pinatubo volcano in the Philippines, for instance, reflected sunlight and cut the global average temperature by about 1 degree in 1992. But that small drop was accompanied by record low temperatures that effectively aborted summer in much of the Northeastern United States and Upper Midwest.

"The extreme events that accompany moderate global change may be more dramatic and important than the small change in the global average," said Dr. James E. Hansen, a climatologist who directs the NASA Goddard Institute for Space Studies in New York.

It is unclear what causes climatic triggers to trip suddenly. Some scientists say abrupt shifts in atmospheric circulation could be responsible. But the most favored candidate appears to be a change in the strength of great ocean currents that transport heat, or even a temporary cessation of the currents.

One way in which this might happen is that an atmosphere that had already begun to warm could produce more precipitation and melt more ice and snow in Arctic areas. That could flood with fresh water the critical current that transports heat to the North Atlantic, diluting the salt content on which the current's functioning depends. With this heat-conveying current halted or greatly weakened, parts of the North Atlantic region, especially Europe, could become much colder than today. One study, reported in *Nature*, suggested that the current could shut down altogether if atmospheric concentrations of carbon dioxide doubled within 100 years, as many scientists believe is inevitable.

"It's kind of ironic," Dr. Taylor said, "but it's possible that the greenhouse warming we are likely to be producing now may lead to a warming period followed by a dramatic cold period."

—WILLIAM K. STEVENS, January 1998

Violent Weather Battering Globe Baffles Experts

THE EXTREME WEATHER OF 1992 and 1993 in North America is part of a worldwide pattern, scientists say, and they are searching hard for an explanation.

The United States has suffered through the extra-cold summer that chilled the Northeast in 1992; Hurricane Andrew in August 1992, the most destructive American hurricane ever; the East Coast "storm of the century" in March 1993; the devastating flooding in the upper Midwest that summer; and the seemingly unending snows of early 1994 in the Northeast, accompanied by record warmth in the West.

All are part of a global pattern of sharper climatic swings over about the last decade, say climatologists. Around the world, the 1980s and early 1990s were remarkable for the "frequency and intensity of extremes of weather and climate," Dr. John Houghton, a cochairman of an international group of scientists advising the United Nations on climate change, says in the book *Global Warming: The Complete Briefing* (Lion Publishing, Oxford, England).

One tempting explanation for the extreme weather would be to ascribe it to the start of global warming, the feared climate change that could be brought about by emissions of heat-trapping industrial waste gases. Computer models of global climate predict more violent weather as the atmosphere heats up. But most climatologists say the small amount of warming seen so far could well lie within the normal limits of the climate's variability. And whatever the cause of the warming, it may or may not be responsible for the recent climatic extremes, says Dr. Houghton: "We have no means of knowing, actually."

If global warming cannot be blamed for the two-year blast of violent weather, scientists must turn to the usual suspects, such as the circulation of air currents, the positioning of storm systems and the distribution of heat and moisture. These are the factors that determine weather on a local and regional scale, and the puzzle is to see if there is some new interconnection that has driven them to their recent round of assaults.

While scientists have no definitive answers, some clues have come their way. They have found, for instance, that some large-scale patterns of air circulation may come and go in a rough kind of cycle. The average winter course of the North American jet stream, along which storms develop, has recently shifted from a relatively straight west-to-east path across the continent to a curvier one that dips south from the Pacific Northwest into the central part of the country and then turns upward through the Middle Atlantic states.

This curvier pattern allows colder, wetter weather to plunge down into the Northeast and warmer, drier weather to thrust upward into the West. The jet stream broke sharply from a flatter pattern in the late 1950s and the curvy pattern has predominated ever since, according to studies by Dr. Daniel J. Leathers of the University of Delaware and Dr. Michael A. Palecki of the State University of New York at Buffalo. Variations on the pattern are believed partly responsible both for 1993's many winter snowstorms in the Northeast and for a period of more intense northeasters in the Middle Atlantic states.

The pattern is itself linked to sea-surface temperatures in the Pacific Ocean, and especially to the behavior of one of the globe's most powerful weather makers: the cycle featuring El Niño, a quasiperiodic oscillation in which temperatures in the tropical Pacific rise above average, then fall below it over irregular periods of two to seven years. The changes in ocean temperature touch off long-distance atmospheric chain reactions that alter patterns of air circulation and often bring drought or excessive rains to various parts of the world. El Niño, the warming phase of the cycle, is believed to have been a factor in causing Midwestern floods in 1993.

El Niño events have become relatively more frequent in the last 15 to 20 years, and Dr. Leathers and Dr. Palecki found that the curvy North American jet stream comes and goes in an approximate rhythm with them and other changes in Pacific sea-surface temperatures.

Similar processes may be at work in other parts of the globe. But all of this amounts to a snippet of understanding, given the vast complexity of the climate system. What seems clearer is that the system has been serving up more extremes and greater variability over the last decade or so.

Dr. Houghton cites insurance-industry figures that show that the number of catastrophic windstorms worldwide in the 1980s was 29—more than double the 14 of the 1970s, which had in turn increased from the eight of the 1960s. Insured losses from these storms have increased tenfold since the 1960s. Some of the increase is related to more people living in the storm-struck areas, but much of it "seems to have arisen from the increased storminess in the late 1980s and early 1990s," Dr. Houghton says. Moreover, floods and droughts have been going to extremes as well, he says.

Some of the extreme weather may be linked to El Niño, Dr. Houghton, chief executive of the Meteorological Office of Britain until his retirement in 1991, and other climatologists say. A 1982 to 1983 El Niño event was one of the strongest on record and caused climatic devastation from California to South America to Australia. An unusually cold turn of the cycle, the opposite side of the coin that has been named La Niña, has been tied, though inconclusively, to both the Bangladesh floods and the Midwestern drought of 1988. And an especially protracted El Niño, lasting for three years and ending only in the last few has been implicated, at least partly, in some of the latest climatic behavior.

One obstacle to further understanding of weather cycles is that good records go back only to the 1940s, said Anthony Barnston, a senior analyst at the National Weather Service Climate Analysis Center at Camp Springs, Maryland. It could be, he said, that "it's run of the mill that we have these decade-to-decade changes in variability," but there is no good way to tell.

Some parts of the climate system, like the El Niño–La Niña cycle, vary on less than a decade's scale and are easier to analyze. Scientists have pinned down pretty well how the cycle affects weather in various parts of the globe through "teleconnections," or chains of cause and effect that ripple through the atmosphere as a result of tropical ocean warming or cooling. But they can only approximate when the cycle will turn, and sometimes, as with everyday weather predictions, they are wrong.

The chief reason is chaos, the inherent unpredictability of weather systems that thwarts attempts at long-range forecasts. Forecasters are attempting to deal with the chaos in the El Niño cycle by running many different computer simulations that predict a range of outcomes. If many of the outcomes are in a narrow cluster suggesting that an El Niño event is on the way, then that "tilts the roulette table" in favor of such a prediction, said Dr. Mark Cane of Columbia University's Lamont-Doherty Earth Observatory, a pioneer in El Niño forecasting.

"If we had the tools we have now, we might have been able to say months or a year ahead that there was a better than even chance" of a strong El Niño in 1982 and 1983, he said. "We could have said there's such a big tilt to the table" that people in areas affected by the climatic ripples emanating from El Niño should take precautions, he added.

Mr. Barnston said a slight majority of forecasters at the Climate Analysis Center believes that the tropical Pacific, after three years of warm El Niño conditions, is moving into a mild cold period characteristic of La Niña. That phase is usually associated with warm winters in the Southeastern United States, colder than normal winters from the Great Lakes to the Pacific Northwest, unsettled winters in the Northeast and Middle Atlantic states and, maybe, summer drought in the country's midsection.

By changing the distribution of storms over the ocean, El Niño creates warmer conditions in the Western United States and cooler ones in the Northeast—the exact pattern of 1993's winter. This effect has tended to be more prevalent since about 1976, when a period of relatively more frequent El Niño events began, said Dr. Kevin Trenberth, a climate researcher at the Center for Atmospheric Research in Boulder, Colorado. "What happened this past winter in some sense was another example that fits into that particular phase," he said.

Climatologists are only beginning to try to understand how all the factors influencing climate fit together. Many are sure, however, that global greenhouse warming, if and when it happens, will alter atmospheric circulation by creating heat imbalances on the planet's surface: the ocean warms more slowly than the land.

It cools more slowly, too, as when Mount Pinatubo in the Philippines erupted in 1991, cooling the Earth by casting aloft sulfate droplets that reflected sunlight. Some climate researchers believe this imbalance affected weather patterns by altering atmospheric circulation, but they have not yet pinned this down.

Many climatologists believe further that a warmer world will increase the evaporation of ocean water and thereby the number and intensity of storms. Floods, droughts and storms, in other words, would be the likely signature of global warming. And that violent regime could be triggered, some fear, by just a small warming of global climate.

But for now, climatologists are in a dense fog as to whether the recent phase of violent weather is a harbinger of a warming planet or just a normal fluctuation of the global climate.

—WILLIAM K. STEVENS, May 1994

In Ancient Ice Ages, Clues to Climate

MORE OFTEN THAN not over the last million years, the Earth has been locked in the deep cold of ice ages. In the frigid depths of the most recent of these glaciations, which lasted about 100,000 years and ended about 10,000 years ago, great sheets of ice buried much of Europe and North America, including New York, Chicago and everything to the north. In its expansion phase, the ice sometimes advanced so fast that it bulldozed forests in its path.

Most experts believe the ice will come again, as surely as the Earth turns on its axis and revolves around the sun. It will crush cities, freeze great stretches of northern lands and suck up so much of the world's water that global sea levels will drop by hundreds of feet. In some spots, the Northeast Coast will be as much as 100 miles east of where it is now, as it was during the last glaciation. People will survive just as they did then, but the warm, salubrious, all-too-brief interval in which civilization flowered will be over.

The question is: when?

Until recently, scientists who study past glaciations for clues to the future thought the present warm period was nearing its end. Though global warming from the emission of heat-trapping greenhouse gases might complicate the situation, they believed that an uneven slide into a new glaciation could begin at almost any time.

"Now most people have dropped that view," said Dr. Lloyd Burckle, a paleooceanographer at Columbia University's Lamont-Doherty Earth Observatory, who is an expert on ancient climates. Recent evidence has led scientists to believe that the present warm period could last another 10,000 to 20,000 years, or even longer.

They say the evidence, in the form of chemical tracers of past climates contained in deep-ocean sediments, suggests that previous warm periods lasted longer than had been thought. In particular, a warm interval some

400,000 years ago appears to have endured for 30,000 years or more. Scientists call it Stage 11, after its designation in the standard record of glacial-interglacial cycles discovered through study of the deep-sea sediment tracers.

In some critical aspects, Stage 11 appears to have more in common with today's interglacial, denoted as Stage 1 and known as the Holocene period, than do other warm periods of the past.

Dr. David Hodell, a paleooceanographer at the University of Florida, who has produced some of the new evidence on Stage 11, said, "If Stage Eleven is a good analog and lasted thirty thousand years, we might expect that the present interglacial will continue for another twenty thousand years."

Further evidence also suggests that the most recent warm period before the Holocene began about 130,000 years ago and lasted some 20,000 years, twice as long as had been thought—and twice as long as the Holocene has endured so far. That interglacial, sometimes called the Eemian period, appears to have had two distinct phases. One, roughly the first 12,000 years, was warm and stable. The second half of the period saw a gradual growth of ice sheets in the North Atlantic region—but the climate of the region apparently stayed warm for another 8,000 years or so before descending fitfully into a new glaciation.

The evident lag between the growth of ice sheets and their impact on climate is an indication that even if the Earth's overall climate stays warm for another 10,000 to 20,000 years, there may still be severe weather changes. For instance, the intensity of storms in the temperate zones is determined by the contrast in temperature between clashing warm and cold air masses. In the latter part of the last interglacial, some scientists theorize, the juxtaposition of cold, growing ice sheets with a still-warm ocean could have produced monster storms.

How the climate behaved in the earlier warm intervals is one of many mysteries that today plague and fascinate those who study the ice ages. The conundrum is complicated all the more by the potential impact of humans' burning of fossil fuels like coal, oil and natural gas, which produces the heat-trapping atmospheric gas carbon dioxide.

According to a calculation by Dr. James F. Kasting of Pennsylvania State University, an expert on geochemical processes and ancient climate, fossil fuels would be used up in about 800 years at present rates of burning. If that happened, he said, there would be four to eight times as much carbon dioxide in the atmosphere as in preindustrial times, and it would raise the Earth's average surface temperature by 8 to 27 degrees Fahrenheit. "It looks like we would completely break the glacial-interglacial cycle," he said.

That much warming would probably melt all or most of the ice on Earth, raising sea level to heights unknown in the last 65 million years or so and wiping out most of today's coastal zones, where about half of humanity lives. It would probably make the Tropics uninhabitable and return the world's climate to conditions that prevailed in the era of the dinosaurs, when crocodiles lived in the Arctic.

"It's hard to believe we'd ever be that stupid," said Dr. Wallace S. Broecker, a geochemist at Lamont-Doherty. On the other hand, there has so far been little progress in reducing the use of fossil fuels. The peak of whatever global warming might eventually result would come well before the end of the Holocene if, as scientists now suspect, it still has thousands of years yet to run.

The dominant view among scientists is that if greenhouse gas emissions are not reduced, the average global temperature will rise by 2 to 6 degrees Fahrenheit, with a best estimate of 3.5 degrees, over the next century—and that further warming would take place after that if emissions continued. By comparison, the average temperature has risen by 5 to 9 degrees since the depths of the last glaciation some 20,000 years ago.

Some scientists believe the current glacial-interglacial cycle was set in motion more than 2.5 million years ago by the gradual closing of the isthmus of Panama, which rerouted oceanic currents that carry water—and heat—around the globe. Others say the cause was the rise about then of the Himalayas, resulting in a realignment of atmospheric circulation. In any event, the changes had vast repercussions. Until about a million years ago, the alternating glacial and interglacial cycles were of roughly even duration. Since then, the glacial cycles have dominated.

The reigning theory about what sets the timing of the glacial-interglacial oscillations says it involves periodic changes in the Earth's orbit and its position relative to the sun. In one type of periodic change, the angle of tilt in the Earth's axis varies over periods of about 41,000 years. In another, the magnitude of a wobble in the Earth's rotation about that axis (much like that of a spinning top as it slows down) changes over periods of 19,000 and 23,000 years. In a third cycle, the shape of the Earth's orbit varies, from more circular to more elliptical, over a period of 100,000 years.

In theory, the overlapping effect of the three orbital cycles alters the angles and distances from which sunlight strikes the far northern latitudes of the Earth. When less sunlight falls there, less snow melts in summer and over time is compressed to form growing continental ice sheets. When more sunlight falls, the ice melts back.

This elegant theory has been confirmed, in its adherents' view, by studies of the relative abundance of different forms of oxygen preserved in the fossilized shells of tiny marine animals called foraminifera, or forams, in deep-sea sediments around the world.

From the foram record, scientists worked out a timetable of the waning and waxing of ice sheets. They found that it neatly matched the timetable calculated by astronomers on the basis of the Earth's orbital cycles.

Later evidence, however, has suggested that the coming and going of the ice is sometimes out of phase with the global or regional climate. That is, it might remain warm for some time even as ice sheets grow, as in the Eemian period.

Dr. George Kukla of Lamont-Doherty, Dr. Jerry McManus of the Woods Hole Oceanographic Institution in Woods Hole, Massachusetts, and others have documented this lag by studying ocean sediments in the North Atlantic. They looked for concentrations of gravelly debris dropped by melting sea ice and fossils of a species of foram that is sensitive to sea-surface temperature.

The researchers found that after the Eemian interglacial had lasted some 12,000 years, a warm climate persisted in the North Atlantic region for about another 8,000 years, even as the ice concentrations continued to grow. Dr. Kukla says that in the last half of the last interglacial, the ice probably built up gradually in volume, but not necessarily in area, while the ocean and the continental temperate zones remained warm. Then the cold moved south, probably in a series of pulses.

Dr. McManus says the North Atlantic region may have stayed warm for so long because great ocean currents that transport heat into the region remained strong. When the currents weakened, possibly because their salt content was diluted at a critical juncture by fresh water from melting icebergs, a global glaciation began. It lasted some 100,000 years, ending about 10,000 years ago.

If the Holocene behaves like the last interglacial, Dr. Kukla and Dr. McManus say, then the next onset of the cold associated with an ice age lies thousands of years in the future.

As the World Turns

Today's global climate may seem normal, but in fact the last 10,000 years have been just a brief episode of warmth in a million-year era dominated by ice ages. Scientists used to think the present warm period was nearing its end, but now they believe it may last thousands of years more.

THE ASTRONOMICAL THEORY
A favored explanation for the alternation of glacial and interglacial intervals is the effect of astronomical cycles, which combine to alter the amount of sunlight received in far northern latitudes in summer.

ECCENTRICITY
The shape of the Earth's orbit varies, from more circular to more elliptical, putting Earth closer to or farther from the sun.

TILT
Earth's axis of rotation is tilted. The degree of inclination varies above and below 23 degrees.

PRECESSION
Like a spinning top as it slows down, the axis of rotation wobbles, changing the Earth's orientation to the sun.

A Glacial Age Under Way
When less sunlight falls in the far north in summers, snow compacts into ice over millennia. When more sunlight falls, ice melts back.

Tracing the Past
Adherents of the astronomical theory say it has been confirmed by chemical clues found in fossilized shells of tiny marine animals called foraminifera. These shells differ in their proportions of two kinds of oxygen. During glaciations, they are enriched with oxygen-18 because oxygen-16, a lighter form, evaporates from the oceans and is trapped in glacial ice.

But a number of experts are beginning to believe that the length of the Stage 11 interglacial may be a better predictor of how long the Holocene will last. As Dr. Hodell explains, the shape of the Earth's orbit in Stage 11 was more circular then and is similarly so today. The planet's spinning-top wobble was also less pronounced then and is so now.

Together, the two cycles are allowing less solar radiation to reach far northern latitudes in the summer, meaning that less ice is melting each year as a result of the sun's direct action than melted 9,000 years ago: the die is cast for the next glaciation, but according to the new thinking, the world will stay warm for about 10,000 to 20,000 more years.

Much more must be learned before scientists can be confident of what happened in Stage 11, and what that might portend for humanity. Was it warm enough then to melt the ice caps, as some scientists believe? How did the climate vary over the 20 or 30 millenniums that Stage 11 apparently lasted? Firm answers will come only with difficulty, if then.

"If it was a nice neat story," says Dr. McManus, "we'd have known it a long time ago and would have moved on to something else."

—WILLIAM K. STEVENS, February 1999

5

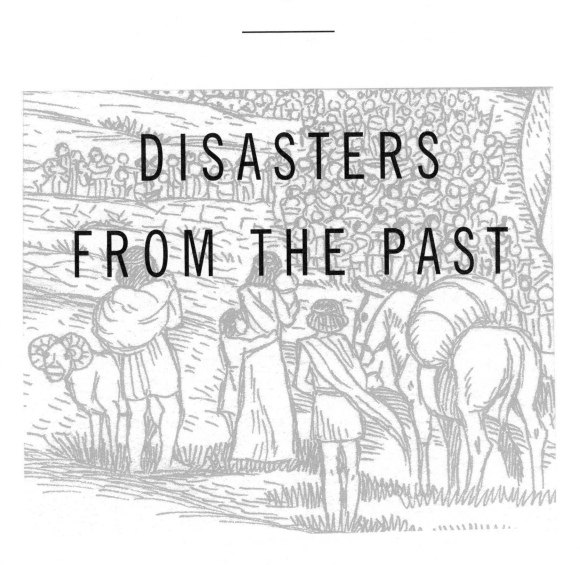

DISASTERS FROM THE PAST

The natural disasters of recorded history are the mildest of pinpricks compared to those that have occurred in distant geological eras and will doubtless recur sometime in the far future.

The great disasters of the past were so disruptive that each wiped out a large proportion of the world's plant and animal species. The fossil record bears witness to the extent of these mass extinctions, about seven of which have occurred since the beginning of life on Earth.

Destroying a species throughout the extent of its range is not so easy. The mass exinctions are assumed to have been caused by widespread disuption of habitat. The impact of large asteroids or comets is one possible cause of the fossil record's mass extinctions. These fearsome events would kick up massive clouds of rock dust into the stratosphere, veiling the sun's light for years and curbing plant growth throughout the planet.

Another possible cause is large-scale volcanism. A single eruption, like that of Tambora, can measurably affect global climate. With many volcanoes belching away during periods of intense volcanism, the climate could be even more seriously chilled. In addition, the lava flows from intense volcanos can cover enormous areas, as shown by the Deccan Traps of India.

One intriguing theory is that large asteroid impacts could set up volcanism at the opposite side of the Earth. Another possibility is that the deep plumes of rock known to cause hot spots, like the one under the Hawaian island chain, could be responsible for volcanic flood plains like the Deccan Traps.

Mass extinctions occur tens of millions of years apart, so there is no particular reason to fear one tomorrow. Equally, there is no basis for assuming there will never be another.

The recent past holds evidence of other titanic disasters, short of mass extinction. These include the Tunguska explosion of 1908, now thought to have been caused by a stony meteorite, and the eruption at Santorini in the Aegean Sea, believed to have destroyed the Minoan civilization of Crete and to have created the legend of Atlantis.

Theory Would Reconcile Rival
Views on Dinosaurs' Demise

IN THE LAST DECADE OR SO two main schools of thought have clashed furiously over the question of what did in the dinosaurs. One school holds that a massive object from outer space slammed into the Earth, kicking up a worldwide pall of dust that blotted out the sun and killed off many plants and animals. The other school prefers to seek the cause of the global mayhem in natural processes like big volcanic eruptions.

Each side has accumulated a lot of evidence to support its case, though lately the advocates of an asteroid collision seem to have had the upper hand.

Now, however, an elegant theory has been proposed that neatly combines both conflicting ideas into a single mechanism.

It posits that a speeding rock from outer space, exploding on collision with the force of millions of hydrogen bombs, would have shot gargantuan shock waves through the Earth. The waves would have coalesced at the side opposite to the impact crater, an area known as the antipode, breaking the ground there and heating it and triggering huge volcanic outflows. Both the impact and its repercussions in the other hemisphere, the theory goes, would have contributed to the mysterious decline of the dinosaurs and many other species some 65 million years ago.

Antipodal volcanism, as the theory is sometimes called, was first discussed in relation to the dinosaurs in the early 1990s and is now taking on new weight as computer modeling begins to suggest its plausibility and as planetary scientists keep finding apparent examples of it in the heavens.

Dr. David A. Williams and Dr. Ronald Greeley of Arizona State University reported in the journal *Icarus* that the largest impact basin on Mars, Hellas Plenitia, is antipodal to Alba Patera, an eruption that sprawls for

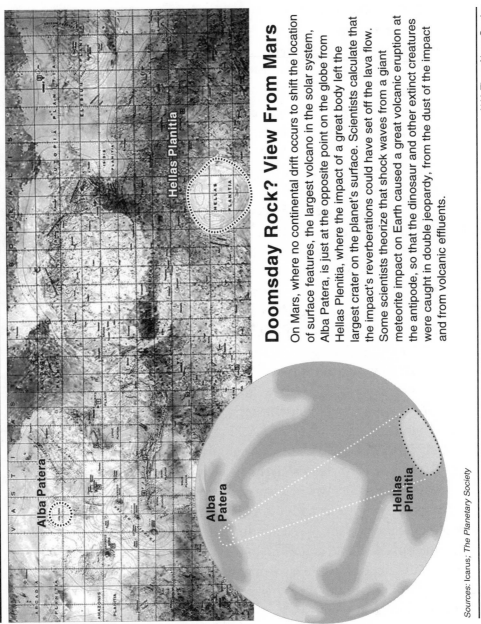

Alba Patera

Hellas Planitia

Doomsday Rock? View From Mars

On Mars, where no continental drift occurs to shift the location of surface features, the largest volcano in the solar system, Alba Patera, is just at the opposite point on the globe from Hellas Plenitia, where the impact of a great body left the largest crater on the planet's surface. Scientists calculate that the impact's reverberations could have set off the lava flow. Some scientists theorize that shock waves from a giant meteorite impact on Earth caused a great volcanic eruption at the antipode, so that the dinosaur and other extinct creatures were caught in double jeopardy, from the dust of the impact and from volcanic effluents.

Alba Patera

Hellas Planitia

Sources: Icarus; The Planetary Society

N.Y. Times News Service

nearly 1,000 miles across the Martian surface and is the largest volcano in the solar system. Moreover, they calculate that the impact's reverberations at the antipode were strong enough to tear open fractures more than 10 miles deep, perhaps helping to trigger a titanic flow of lava.

As for the Earth, a team of scientists at the Sandia National Laboratory in Albuquerque, New Mexico, recently used a powerful computer to simulate the damage a speeding asteroid some six miles in diameter—the estimated size of the dinosaur killer—would have wrought at the impact's antipode. They discovered that the crust there would have heaved as high as 60 feet in a series of catastrophic tremors. In comparison, the ground at the great San Francisco earthquake of 1906 moved a few feet at most.

"The Earth acts like a lens," said Dr. Mark B. Boslough, a Sandia physicist who is leading the simulation effort. "It focuses the energy. There's been a lot of speculation about this in relation to asteroid impacts and volcanic eruptions, but we've done the first rigorous modeling to show where the energy actually goes."

Dr. John T. Hagstrum, an early advocate of the theory who works at the United States Geological Survey in Menlo Park, California, cautioned that antipodal volcanism was far from proved even though it has taken on new substance.

"It explains a lot of coincidences," Dr. Hagstrum said. "I think it has merit. But it could fall flat on its face. Right now, I'm waiting for the smoking gun. I'd call the whole thing intriguing."

The idea that a doomsday rock did in the dinosaurs was first proposed in 1980 by Dr. Walter Alvarez, a geologist at the University of California at Berkeley. He and his colleagues had found unusually large amounts of the rare metal iridium in sediments laid down about the time the dinosaurs died out, at the end of the Cretaceous period. They proposed that the iridium came from a cosmic catastrophe.

A weak link in the theory was the lack of a crater of the correct size and age. But then scientists identified a giant scar more than 100 miles across on the northern edge of the Yucatán Peninsula in Mexico, long buried by erosion and sedimentation. It is now the leading candidate for the impact crater.

But skeptics called the crater evidence shaky and said the extinctions were probably earthly rather than extraterrestrial in origin. Dr. Charles B.

Officer and Dr. Charles L. Drake of Dartmouth College found that the iridium layer was deposited over a period of up to 100,000 years and could have come from large volcanic eruptions originating deep within the Earth. Volcanoes also release chlorine, sulfur dioxide and carbon dioxide, all of which can seriously disrupt the atmosphere.

The dinosaur extinctions, the two scientists noted, occurred around the time that a huge eruption in what is now India created a great lava field known as the Deccan Traps.

Other experts generalized on the volcanic idea, finding that nine of the 10 greatest mass extinctions of all time—including that of the dinosaurs—more or less coincided with enormous floods of lava in various parts of the world.

The link between the two schools of dinosaur extinction is being constructed from well-known scientific principles. For instance, geologists have long known that strong earthquakes send out shock waves that propagate through the Earth and focus at the quake's antipode. Indeed, the phenomenon has been exploited to study the Earth's deep interior.

The geologic focusing is similar to what happens in a large room with a domed roof. A person whispering on one side can sometimes be heard clearly on the other as sound waves bounce off the curve and are focused. So, too, shock waves that radiate outward through the Earth are reflected from the crust and bent by materials of differing density that make up the planet's mantle and core.

Celestial evidence has also come into play. Starting in the early 1970s, astronomers began to identify areas on the moon, Mercury, and icy satellites where impact craters were antipodal to volcanoes and unusual patches of broken crust.

Taken with such evidence, Dr. Hagstrum of Geological Survey and a colleague, Dr. Brent D. Turrin, in 1991 published a outline of the antipodal extinction idea, suggesting that giant bombardments over the eons had touched off heavy volcanic flows, with the linked upheavals combining to cause mass extinctions. But evidence was hard to assemble. Weathering of the Earth's surface over the ages tended to rub out craters, and the constant rearrangement of land masses and ocean beds by the action of plate tectonics made it difficult to ascertain with confidence the exact positions of lava flows and known craters over many millions of years.

Dr. Hagstrum theorized that 65 million years ago, during the great dying-off of the dinosaurs, the Deccan Traps of India were antipodal not to the Yucatán Peninsula where the great crater lies but to a spot in what is now the eastern Pacific Ocean. And the seabed there, he wrote, bears some evidence of a major impact.

Perhaps, some experts suggested, two or more celestial objects hit the Earth simultaneously.

The theorizing was joined in 1992 by Dr. Michael R. Rampino, an Earth scientist at New York University, and Dr. Ken Caldeira, a geologist at Pennsylvania State University. In a paper, they concluded that hot spots within the Earth that are responsible for enormous lava floods tend to occur in antipodal pairs, suggesting that they might have been triggered by cosmic bombardments.

Recent work has been done by the Sandia group, which in addition to Dr. Boslough includes Dr. Eric P. Chael, Dr. T. G. Turcano and Dr. David A. Crawford. In October 1994, they presented a paper on their simulation work at a scientific symposium in Santa Fe, New Mexico.

A six-mile-wide asteroid hitting the Earth at a speed of 45,000 miles per hour, they said, would have dug out a colossal crater that a few seconds after impact would have measured more than 15 miles deep. Top pressures generated by the impacting asteroid would have been about six million times greater than the force exerted by the Earth's atmosphere.

It would have taken about 80 minutes for the shock waves rippling through the Earth from this catastrophe to travel by various routes to the antipode, where they would have converged in a series of catastrophic waves that shook the upper 100 miles or so of the Earth's crust, creating a pipeline of destruction from the depths to the surface.

In an interview, Dr. Boslough said the team had yet to do the computer simulations of how much of the mechanical energy of the gargantuan waves would have been turned into heat and melting of rocks, possibly triggering large-scale volcanism. But he said the antipodal stimulus appeared to be enough to trigger major upheavals.

The heat calculations, he said, might take another year and required the use of supercomputers at Sandia, which is an arm of the Department of Energy. Until then, he said, caution was the watchword.

New Proof of Asteroid's Devastation

SCIENTISTS PROBING THE DEEP SEA have found the best evidence yet of distant turmoil wrought by a gargantuan asteroid that slammed into Earth 65 million years ago. The finding is expected to shed new light on the wave of global extinction and repopulation that swept the planet at the end of the age of dinosaurs.

The speeding mountain of rock from outer space hit the Gulf of Mexico and carved out a huge crater, which is known today as Chicxulub. It also blasted an inferno of white-hot debris into the sky that probably rained down for days and weeks around the globe. Over the ages, geological processes like erosion and sedimentation have often jumbled or diluted such faraway clues of planetary mayhem.

Now, however, scientists penetrating through nearly two miles of sea and seabed with drilling equipment have found clear evidence of just how badly the Chicxulub asteroid shook the foundations of the planet.

"In my view, this really nails it down," Dr. Robert W. Corell, head of geosciences at the National Science Foundation, a federal agency that financed the research, said in an interview.

Scientists aboard the *Resolution*, the world's largest research ship—run by JOIDES, the Joint Oceanographic Institutions for Deep Earth Sampling, a consortium of international scientific groups—just returned from a monthlong voyage in which they lowered a long pipe to drill into the seabed 1.6 miles down. The investigation site, about 300 miles off northern Florida, was 1,000 miles or so from the Chicxulub crater, which extends beneath the northern tip of the Yucatán Peninsula.

From a depth of about 370 feet beneath the seabed, the *Resolution* pulled up a 16-inch-long, muddy layer cake of distinct bands revealing the evolution of the cosmic catastrophe.

One of the expedition leaders, Dr. Richard D. Norris, a paleobiologist at the Woods Hole Oceanographic Institution in Massachusetts, said the core was extraordinary because of the clarity and comprehensiveness of its bands.

The first, and oldest, shows ancient planktonic life in the sea before the asteroid struck, the second shows a jumble of rubble from melted terrestrial rock thrown skyward by the asteroid, the third shows the rusty debris of the asteroid itself, the fourth shows a dead layer of gray clay, and the last shows teeming life.

Scientists say the latter layer, two to four inches thick, will likely prove important for gaining insights into how tiny organisms and other survivors of the planetary inferno repopulated the seas. The explosion of new life occurred relatively quickly, the experts note, with the dead zone lasting about 5,000 years or so.

"You can see these really minute but beautifully preserved fossils," Dr. Norris said in an interview. "It is amazing how quickly the new species appeared."

—WILLIAM J. BROAD, February 1997

"It's hard not to like the theory, but you don't want to get carried away," he said. "You have to do the rigorous modeling and you have to believe what the modeling says." He also said a wide range of field studies could be pursued to try to detect antipodal clues.

Reaction to the theory generally seems to be one of interest among scientific generalists, although die-hards of both extinction camps are said to be skeptical of almost any idea that ventures to reconcile the conflicting schools.

"The more extreme members of the volcanism crowd are not very open to anything from outside of the Earth," said Dr. Clark R. Chapman, a senior scientist at the Planetary Science Institute in Tucson, Arizona, and a backer of the impact hypothesis. "An open-minded person would just wait to see how the evidence plays out. To me, it's a very intriguing possibility."

—WILLIAM J. BROAD, December 1994

Many Small Events May Add Up to One Mass Extinction

DID THE MASS EXTINCTIONS THAT have punctuated the history of life on this planet have a common cause, or were they just statistical fluctuations nudged to extremes by many unrelated causes?

Since 1980, heated scientific debates have arisen from this and related questions. Many disagreements have centered on the wave of extinctions at the end of the Cretaceous period some 65 million years ago that saw the demise of the dinosaurs, the marine shellfish called ammonites and many other large groups of animals.

Partisans of various opposing theories have argued that major mass extinctions throughout the 3.5-billion-year history of life on Earth have been caused by the impact of large meteors, by volcanic eruptions that covered an area the size of a continent, by protracted ice ages, by changes in sea level, epidemics and many other factors.

But a collaboration of European scientists has raised another possibility: mass extinctions may be caused by complex, interacting conditions that cannot be encompassed by any simple explanation.

The scientists reported in the journal *Nature* that their analysis of data culled from the fossil record reveals statistical patterns over time that mathematicians describe as "fractal." In this kind of pattern, the frequency of an event taking place is inversely proportional to its intensity; for example, the statistical expectation is that there will be a certain number of small earthquakes for every large one.

The report suggests that extinctions of all magnitudes, from the smallest to the most devastating, probably had many different causes and that future mass extinctions may be intrinsically unpredictable.

Moreover, the impact of an asteroid or a continental blast of volcanic lava may not be needed to kill off a large proportion of the Earth's animals and plants, the authors said; relatively small changes in global conditions may sometimes combine in complex ways to precipitate catastrophic consequences.

There is growing evidence that the mass extinction at the end of the Cretaceous period occurred about the same time that a monster meteor struck the Yucatán Peninsula. And yet, efforts to link other major extinctions with similar impacts have largely failed.

One of the authors of the *Nature* paper, Dr. Michael J. Benton, a paleontologist at the University of Bristol, England, said in an interview that he believes the Cretaceous extinction was the only one of the "big five" mass extinctions for which there is fairly good evidence that a large meteor impact occurred about the same time. (The other four occurred at the end of the Cambrian period 500 million years ago, at the end of the Devonian period 350 million years ago, at the end of the Permian period 230 years ago—the most devastating of all—and at the end of the Triassic period 195 million years ago.)

Moreover, there are several meteor craters of about the same size as the Yucatán crater (110 miles in diameter) that do not correspond in time to any known mass extinction, Dr. Benton said.

The European study was headed by Ricard V. Sole, a physicist at the Polytechnic University of Catalonia, Barcelona, with his student, Susanna C. Manrubia, with Dr. Benton and Dr. Per Bak, a physicist at the Niels Bohr Institute in Copenhagen, Denmark.

The European scientists who conducted the study culled statistics from the fossil record and concluded that extinctions large and small fit a fractal pattern known as "scale-invariant self-similarity." This means, roughly, that a common statistical pattern pervades a certain class of things, regardless of how the size scale varies.

According to ideas pioneered by a French mathematician, Dr. Benoit Mandelbrot, fractal patterns manifest themselves throughout nature. Thus, the jagged pattern of a shoreline seems much the same at all scales, whether viewed in fine detail from an inch above or in gross outline a mile above.

In the European study, the supposed fractal scale is based on increments of time during which extinctions took place. The scientists plotted patterns of extinctions over different time scales, and found that the patterns over large intervals of time seemed similar (although different in scale) to patterns within smaller time scales. They conclude that the erratic responses of the Earth's "biosphere" to perturbations—including small ones, like the normal fluctuations in the ratios between competing species "provide the main mechanism for the distribution of extinction events."

This neither supports nor weakens any particular theory on how the dinosaurs or any other group became extinct. Mathematically speaking, Dr. Benton said, it is equally possible for an extinction to have been the result of the internal dynamics of an ecosystem, or an asteroid impact, or any other influence.

But as scientists try to discern a coherent pattern underlying the mass extinctions, doesn't the new report amount to a frustrating return to the starting line?

"Yes, I think that's right," Dr. Benton said. "I think the mathematics are perfectly concordant with the idea of all kinds of crises contributing to extinctions, with no explanation particularly favored."

Among the critics of this view is Dr. David M. Raup, a statistical paleontologist who retired several years ago from the University of Chicago.

Dr. Raup has argued for more than a decade that most extinctions—minor waves as well as globally catastrophic ones—result from meteor impacts. The quest for subtle biological interactions and for complex mathematical models to explain how they can add up to mass extinctions is futile, he said, because the evidence is that some 60 percent of all extinctions are caused by extraterrestrial matter: comets, asteroids and other small objects.

Regarding Dr. Bak's notion that extinctions occur in fractal patterns independently of specific causes, Dr. Raup said in an interview: "It's intuitively wonderful. A very cuddly idea. But I don't buy it."

Statistical explanations of this kind remind him, he said, of the ideas of Dr. Rene Thom, a French mathematician whose "Catastrophe Theory" was popularized in the 1970s as a mathematical model for explaining the abrupt onset of wars, traffic jams, stock crashes, chemical reactions and much more.

Catastrophe theory was based on analyses of the topology, or surface structure, of abstract mathematical shapes endowed with "cusps." These cusps, like the tips of upward pointing needles, were places where an object could be sent flying with equal probability in several possible directions, with the slightest push.

"Physicists' theories that attempt to explain everything can end up explaining nothing," he said.

—MALCOLM W. BROWNE, September 1997

Santorini Volcano Ash, Traced Afar, Gives a Date of 1623 B.C.

ASH BELIEVED TO BE from a great explosive eruption that buried the Minoan colony on the island of Santorini 36 centuries ago has been extracted from deep in an ice core retrieved last year from central Greenland. Its depth in the core indicated that the Aegean eruption, which may have given rise to the Atlantis legend, occurred in or about 1623 B.C.

From the top half of the 9,000-foot core evidence has been found of some 400 volcanic eruptions in the past 7,000 years. The ash spewed into the air was high and voluminous enough to reach Greenland, about 3,500 miles away. A prominent ash layer at a depth corresponding to 4803 B.C. may have come from the eruption in Oregon that destroyed Mount Mazama, leaving the giant caldera that is now Crater Lake.

Results of the analysis were reported in the journal *Science* by Dr. Gregory A. Zielinski of the University of New Hampshire and colleagues at the university and from the Army's Cold Regions Research and Engineering Laboratory in Hanover, New Hampshire, and Pennsylvania State University.

The study was part of the Greenland Ice Sheet Project 2, which extracted an ice core from the entire thickness of ice at Greenland's summit. A second core extracted nearby by a European team is also being analyzed.

Dr. Zielinski took microscopic ash fragments from some of the largest eruptions, including the one believed to have occurred at Santorini, to Queens University in Belfast, Northern Ireland, for analysis. Chemical analysis of ash from the eastern Mediterranean and Black Sea has shown that it all apparently came from the Santorini explosion.

Because wind systems in the Northern and Southern Hemisphere are somewhat independent, most eruptions evident in the Greenland ice have been attributed to volcanoes in the Northern Hemisphere. But there are

143

exceptions. One in about A.D. 177 is believed to have been at Taupo, New Zealand, whose ash may have risen almost 40 miles.

Ash layers in the core have been identified by their sulfur content. Fifty-seven of 69 events recorded for the last 2,000 years were matched with known eruptions. This was true, however, of only 30 percent of the older record, to 7000 B.C.

The Greenland core records 18 huge eruptions that took place from 7,000 to 9,000 years ago, depositing unusually heavy layers of ash. That was when the great ice sheets were melting and, the authors of the *Science* article suggest, may have been when molten material deep within the Earth's volcanic zones welled up in response to the diminishing burden of ice. Those zones included Kamchatka, the Aleutians and Iceland, all up-wind of Greenland or relatively near.

The earliest exactly dated eruption was that of Vesuvius, which destroyed Pompeii and Herculaneum in A.D. 79, preserving their precious frescoes under a blanket of ash. The same thing happened 16 centuries earlier at Santorini, which is also known as Thira. The island was buried under ash that in places was more than 900 feet deep, preserving wall paintings that document in vivid detail the Minoan way of life.

Wall paintings on Crete, the chief Minoan center 75 miles to the south, were not similarly protected from weathering, earthquakes and tidal waves and have been a major restoration challenge.

Ash from the Santorini explosion has already been identified deep in sediment layers on the floor of the Eastern Mediterranean, in Egypt's Nile delta and in parts of the Black Sea. There are also suspicions that its ash cloud persisted long enough to stunt the growth of oak trees in Irish bogs and of bristlecone pines in the White Mountains of California, producing tightly packed tree rings.

Uncovering the buried city on Santorini was first stimulated in the 1860s when it was found that the ash made ideal waterproof cement. Shiploads were exported to build the Suez Canal, but not until 1967 did large-scale excavation of the buried city begin, to be led for many years by Dr. Spyridon Marinatos of Greece.

The demise of the Minoan civilization has long been a mystery and for many years Dr. Marinatos attributed it to ash clouds, earthquakes and tidal waves from the Santorini eruption and the collapse that formed its caldera. More precise datings, however, indicate that the Minoan decline on Crete came many years later.

The eruption, however, was clearly catastrophic and many archeologists believe that flooding and burial of Akrotiri, the Santorini city, could have been the basis for Plato's account of Atlantis. Layering in walls of the Santorini caldera show that it has been the scene of many catastrophic eruptions.

Plato's account is the primary source of the Atlantis legend. He attributed the account to Solon, an Athenian statesman of an earlier century. Many elements of the story seem improbable, such as an attack on Greece 9,000 years earlier by warriors from an island, "Atlantis," in an ocean beyond the Pillars of Hercules (the Strait of Gibraltar). Yet Plato's description of the destroyed island refers to many features, like the pursuit and sacrifice of sacred bulls, that were hallmarks of the Minoan civilization of Crete and Santorini.

The Atlantis invaders, said Plato, were defeated when there were "violent earthquakes and floods; and in a single day and night of misfortune all your warlike body of men in a body sank into the earth, and the island of Atlantis in like manner disappeared in the depths of the sea."

—WALTER SULLIVAN, June 1994

Heavy Volcanic Eras Were Caused by Plumes from the Earth's Core

GEOLOGISTS ON THE TRAIL OF a rare isotope of helium have stumbled on a remarkable finding about the outpourings of lava that every few millions of years or so inundate vast regions of the planet with a sea of fiery rock.

These upheavals, among the most violent natural phenomena on Earth, are important landmarks in geological history because they are associated with the most severe environmental crises, when life was very nearly extinguished from the planet for thousands of years. Their rocky aftermath, known as flood basalts, can exceed by many thousandfold the volume from an ordinary volcanic eruption, like that at Mount St. Helens in 1980.

An international team of geologists and geochemists has looked for chemical clues of eruption ancestry in two of the Earth's biggest flood basalts, in India and Siberia. The team found that the old lava is riddled with tiny bubbles of helium-3—a primordial gas and a signature of the molten underground rock, known as magma, that has risen in long plumes from some 1,800 miles beneath the Earth's surface, near its core.

Scientists have long debated whether flood basalts come from shallow or deep parts of the Earth's hot interior, and the team says this puzzle has now been decisively solved.

"We are proving definitively that it's from the core-mantle boundary," said Dr. Asish R. Basu, the team leader and a geochemist at the University of Rochester. "This answers important questions about the most catastrophic volcanism in the history of our planet."

Conducted over more than five years, the research was performed by scientists at the University of Rochester, the Berkeley Geochronology Center, the United States Geological Survey, the Russian Academy of Sciences

A Shallow Volcano
An ordinary continental volcano stems from shallow geological roots, a bit of crust plunging under another.

Mid-Ocean Vents
Hot vents form where continental plates spread apart in the ocean, but their origin is also comparatively shallow.

An Underground Abscess
Scientists think some plumes were trapped below continents, building up great reservoirs before bursting forth.

Hot Spots and Islands
A deep plume, cutting the thin, moving ocean crust like a blow torch, formed island chains like the Hawaiian Islands.

and the Presidency College in Calcutta, India. The work was discussed most recently in the journal *Science*.

The Siberian flood basalts that the team studied are the planet's largest, having disgorged enough lava to have covered the entire surface of the Earth with up to 10 feet of blistering hot molten rock. The eruptions occurred 250 million years ago, at the end of the Permian era, a time of wrenching global change when up to 97 percent of all the planet's animal and plant species were wiped out, clearing the way for the rise of the dinosaurs.

"What is remarkable is that helium-three is so well preserved in these rocks after two hundred and fifty million years," said Dr. Paul R. Renne, a team member from the Berkeley Geochronology Center. "It's like finding complete DNA preserved in dinosaur fossils."

The Indian eruptions that the team studied took place 65 million years ago, at the end of the Cretaceous period, during another riot of global extinction that did in such creatures as the dinosaurs and cleared the way for the rise of the mammals and man. In debating the cause of such extinctions, some scientists hold that the huge outpourings of lava with their ash and climatic turmoil were responsible. Others lay the blame on the impacts of speeding asteroids and comets that kicked up enough dust to blot out the sun for years.

The new helium-3 work lends support to a possible reconciliation of the competing theories.

The story of the flood basalt origins begins with the most violent outburst of them all—the primordial Big Bang, the theorized explosive birth of the universe more than 10 billion years ago. Primordial helium, most scientists believe, was created in the first two minutes after the Big Bang and became, along with primordial hydrogen, the raw material for all of the early stars and galaxies.

Later, the helium became a building block for the solar system and was widely distributed among the young planets and the sun. It was discovered by astronomers in 1868, when their investigations of the composition of sunlight uncovered some unusual spectral lines. The new element was dubbed "Helios," after the Greek word for sun.

This colorless, tasteless, odorless gas is rare at the Earth's surface because it is so light. Any helium released from a balloon quickly floats out into space. So does helium in porous surface rocks, which tends to dissipate fairly quickly.

Some helium is found in the Earth's crust, but the vast majority of it is not primordial helium-3 but helium-4, an isotope produced by the radioactive decay of the elements uranium and thorium and a source that is constantly replenished. The helium-3 that was once in the crust and the upper Earth has virtually all been removed by eons of melting, erosion and geological recycling.

So scientists were surprised in 1969 when mysterious wisps of primordial helium-3 were discovered in the ocean. Over the next few years, the wisps were traced to the midocean ridges that gird the globe like seams on a baseball and where magma from the Earth's fiery mantle wells up through long gashes.

The helium-3 leaking from the rifts between continental plates had traveled from the Earth's interior and was viewed as a gaseous remnant of the Earth's formation some 4.5 billion years ago and, even earlier, the cosmic Big Bang.

Also in the 1970s, very high levels of helium-3 were discovered spewing out of certain kinds of volcanoes, like those in Hawaii and Iceland. By contrast, far less helium-3 was found in volcanoes on continental margins, like those in the Andes and the Rockies.

In the late 1970s and early 1980s, scientists assembled such clues into a comprehensive picture that held that the Hawaiian-type volcanoes were formed by giant plumes of magma that arose from deep inside the earth at the core-mantle boundary, about 1,800 miles down. By contrast, the continental volcanoes were seen as arising from much shallower roots.

A pioneer of the plume thesis was Dr. W. Jason Morgan of Princeton University, a prominent geophysicist who saw plumes as engines of plate tectonics, the slow churning of the Earth's hot interior that creates, moves and destroys huge chunks of the Earth's crust.

As part of his theorizing, beginning in 1971, Dr. Morgan proposed that hot plumes of magma were responsible for the catastrophic flood basalts. The plumes would form near the Earth's core and travel up through the mantle to burn through the crust to wreak global havoc.

Though it won little attention, Dr. Morgan's surmise caught the eye of Dr. Basu, who was then a graduate student and later became chairman of the department of Earth sciences at the University of Rochester. A geo-chemist, he eventually decided to search for helium-3 in flood basalts, even though colleagues had warned him that such old rocks would harbor none because the light gas would have escaped over the eons.

Meanwhile, the Morgan thesis grew steadily more plausible as the prevalence of giant plumes became well established. It was easy to visual-ize how a great plume, working like a blowtorch, might readily cut through thin ocean crust to produce a series of islands, like the Hawaiian chain. But cutting through the thicker crust of a continental landmass would take much longer, and the results, when they came, would involve the explosive release of a pent-up flood of hot lava.

A native of Calcutta, Dr. Basu and his colleagues began their helium-3 search in the late 1980s and first looked for it at the extensive flood basalts in India known as the Deccan Traps, stairlike layers of lava that cover more than 200,000 square miles, an area bigger than California.

After much trial and error, the team was able to measure helium-3 preserved in tiny basalt bubbles. The secret was finding basaltic rocks that formed at the very start of the Deccan eruptions, before magma from the plume first started breaking through the crust. Unlike the bulk of the Dec-can basalts, these rocks north of the main flows cooled underground and trapped the helium instead of releasing it into the atmosphere.

The helium finding was reported in *Science* by Dr. Basu, Dr. Robert J. Poreda and Friedrich Teichmann of the University of Rochester, Dr. Renne of the Berkeley Geochronology Center in Berkeley, California (formerly named the Institute of Human Origins), and Deb K. DasGupta of Presi-dency College in Calcutta, India.

The discovery, the team wrote, showed that helium isotopes "can be used as tracers for detecting ancient mantle plumes" and for linking the plumes to the formation of flood basalts.

Next Dr. Basu and his colleagues turned their attention northward, to the Siberian flood basalts. Using a similar method developed in India, the team found primordial helium there, too, and reported their findings in *Sci-ence* in an article authored by Dr. Basu, Dr. Poreda, Dr. Renne, Mr. Teich-mann, Dr. Yurii R. Vasiliev and Nikolai V. Sobolev of the Russian Academy of Sciences and Dr. Brent D. Turrin of the United States Geological Survey.

"I see Morgan every year," Dr. Basu said in an interview. "We're simply proving him right."

Since the existence of giant plumes is now a widely accepted part of modern geology, as is their role in the formation of flood basalts, the new findings are seen as evolutionary rather than revolutionary, as generating proofs for existing beliefs.

Even so, some skeptics still hold that the plumes are shallow rather than deep, insisting that the helium-3 readings are ambiguous. Dr. Don L. Anderson, a geophysicist at the California Institute of Technology, says that helium analysis is loaded with complexities and shaky conjectures that can undercut the deep hypothesis.

"Nobody's proved that helium-three is from the core-mantle boundary," Dr. Anderson said in an interview. "It's all based on assumptions." In contrast to the new findings, Dr. Anderson holds that the flood basalts originated at a depth of not more than 250 miles.

Dr. Basu says that Dr. Anderson, as the discoverer of a major geological boundary that exists at a depth of 250 miles, is biased in favor of shallow mechanisms.

If long, deep plumes are indeed responsible for the Earth's flood basalts, as most geologists believe, then this mechanism may help reconcile the competing mass-extinction theories.

Recently, scientists have proposed that a speeding asteroid or comet, colliding with Earth and exploding with the force of millions of hydrogen bombs, might have shot gargantuan shock waves through the globe. The waves would have coalesced at the side opposite the impact crater, an area known as the antipode, breaking the ground there, heating it and triggering huge volcanic outflows. Both the impact and its repercussions in the other hemisphere, the theory goes, would have contributed to the mass extinctions.

A key step in this process, according to the new reasoning, is that shock waves focusing along the axial line through the Earth may have helped trigger the formation of giant plumes to feed the eruptions, which usually occurred over millions of years.

Antipodal volcanism, as the theory is sometimes called, is not widely accepted but is considered an intriguing line of research.

Scientists have already found the remnants of a massive impact crater, in the vicinity of Mexico's Yucatán Peninsula, that has been dated to 65 million years ago, the time of the vast Indian eruptions. It is not antipodal to the Deccan Traps, but scientists are looking for crater evidence in antipodal areas, believing that perhaps two or more celestial objects hit Earth nearly simultaneously.

Dr. Basu is also hunting for evidence of an antipodal impact crater that might have been responsible for the Siberian flood basalts and the great wave of extinction that swept the Earth 250 million years ago, the most terrible of the planetary cataclysms.

"If somebody finds it," he says, "that will pretty much prove that impacts are causing these plumes."

—WILLIAM J. BROAD, August 1995

Study Finds Asteroid Leveled Siberian Area in 1908

A SCIENTIFIC TEAM SAYS IT has solved the mystery of what exploded 84 years ago over Siberia with a force of 1,000 Hiroshima-size nuclear weapons, flattening hundreds of square miles of forest: it was a stony asteroid 100 or so feet in diameter, they say.

For decades experts have debated the cause of the explosion over Tunguska on June 30, 1908. Evidence has always been sparse.

The object exploded about five miles in the air, and no part of it has been found. The shock wave and intense radiant energy flattened trees over an area more than half the size of New York City, and the pressure wave was recorded around the globe.

The cause most often proposed has been a comet plunging into the atmosphere at supersonic speeds. The icy core of a comet was considered so fragile that it would explode high in the atmosphere, leaving no fragments solid enough to dig a crater.

In 1978 L. Kresak, a Czechoslovak scientist, also noted that the explosion coincided with the annual meteor shower that occurs as the Earth passes through the debris of Comet Encke.

The denser celestial objects known as asteroids were also proposed but often dismissed, because an asteroid big enough to produce the blast was envisioned as at least partly surviving and hitting the ground.

Now scientists from the National Aeronautics and Space Administration and the University of Wisconsin, writing in the journal *Nature,* have given the asteroid thesis new weight and rigor.

In a mathematical simulation of the Tunguska explosion, the researchers show that cometary nuclei and carbonaceous asteroids explode far too high to account for the blast, and that iron-rich asteroids tend to explode low and leave craters. The only logical source, they say, is a stony asteroid, the most common type.

"This event represents a typical fate for stony asteroids," wrote Dr. Christopher F. Chyba of the Goddard Space Flight Center in Greenbelt, Maryland, Dr. Paul J. Thomas of the University of Wisconsin at Eau Clair and Dr. Kevin J. Zahnle of Ames Research Center in California.

In the analysis, the team calculated the effects of aerodynamics on the mass that exploded, showing that these forces could easily smash it into fragments that experienced a sharp rise in atmospheric drag and heating.

Thus, the scientists concluded, a 100-foot stony asteroid must have exploded at a height of about five miles in a "catastrophic fragmentation." A smaller stony asteroid would have exploded much higher, the team said, and a larger one would have hit the Earth.

Astronomers believe there are more than a million asteroids with diameters greater than 100 feet whose orbits take them across the path of the Earth, and that Tunguska-type collisions occur every 300 years or so.

Dr. Henry J. Melosh of the Lunar and Planetary Laboratory of the University of Arizona, commenting in *Nature,* said the asteroid team had "wrapped up" the most believable explanation.

Among the remaining mysteries, Dr. Melosh wrote, is why the night skies of Western Europe were strangely bright after the blast. The new findings, he noted, have revived a suggestion that the bright nights were due to sunlight reflected from water-ice clouds created when the Tunguska fireball drove large quantities of wet air into the normally dry upper atmosphere.

—WILLIAM J. BROAD, January 1993

Collapse of Earliest Known Empire Is Linked to Long, Harsh Drought

UNDER THE RENOWNED SARGON AND his successors, the Akkadians of Mesopotamia forged the world's first empire more than 4,300 years ago. They seized control of cities along the Euphrates River and on the fruitful plains to the north, all in what is now Iraq, Syria and parts of southern Turkey. Then, after only a century of prosperity, the Akkadian Empire collapsed abruptly, for reasons that have been lost to history.

The traditional explanation is one of divine retribution. Angered by the hubris of Naram-Sin, Sargon's grandson and most dynamic successor, the gods supposedly unleashed the barbaric Gutians to descend out of the highlands and overwhelm Akkadian towns. More recent and conventional explanations have put the blame on overpopulation, provincial revolt, nomadic incursions or managerial incompetence, though many scholars despaired of ever identifying the root cause of the collapse.

A team of archeologists, geologists and soil scientists has now found evidence that seems to solve the mystery. The Akkadian Empire, they suggest, was beset by a 300-year drought and literally dried up. A microscopic analysis of soil moisture at the ruins of Akkadian cities in the northern farmlands disclosed that the onset of the drought was swift and the consequences severe, beginning about 2200 B.C.

"This is the first time an abrupt climate change has been directly linked to the collapse of a thriving civilization," said Dr. Harvey Weiss, a Yale University archeologist and leader of the American-French research team.

Such a devastating drought would explain the abandonment at that time of Akkadian cities across the northern plain, a puzzling phenomenon observed in archeological excavations. It would also account for the sud-

155

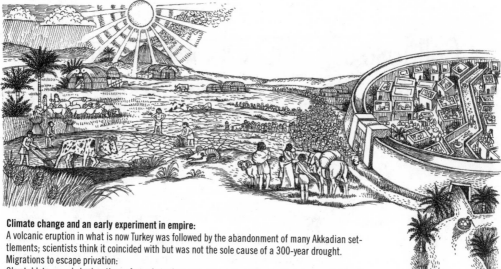

Climate change and an early experiment in empire:
A volcanic eruption in what is now Turkey was followed by the abandonment of many Akkadian settlements; scientists think it coincided with but was not the sole cause of a 300-year drought.
Migrations to escape privation:
Clay tablets recorded migrations of people to the south, where the influx doubled the population of cities, overtaxed food and water supplies and led to civil unrest, fighting and the fall of the dynasty founded by the Akkadian ruler Sargon. Some of the refugees, a group of migratory herders called Amorites, eventually assumed leadership at the rising city of Babylon, founding a great empire.

den migrations of people to the south, as recorded in texts on clay tablets. These migrations doubled the populations of southern cities, overtaxed food and water supplies, and led to fighting and the fall of the Sargon dynasty.

The new findings thus call attention to the role of chance—call it fate, an act of God or simply an unpredictable natural disaster—in the development of human cultures and the rise and fall of civilizations.

Among the drought's refugees were a herding people known as Amorites, characterized by scribes in the city of Ur as "a ravaging people with the instincts of a beast, a people who know not grain"—the ultimate putdown in an economy based on grain agriculture. An 110-mile wall, called the "Repeller of the Amorites," was erected to hold them off. But when the drought finally ended in about 1900 B.C., leadership in the region had passed from Akkad to Ur and then to the Amorites, whose power was centered at the rising city of Babylon. Hammurabi, the great ruler of Babylon in 1800 B.C., was a descendant of Amorites.

The correlation between drastic climate change and the Akkadian downfall also appears to complete the picture of widespread environmental crisis disrupting societies throughout the Middle East in the same centuries. Earlier studies had noted the effects of severe drought, including abandoned towns, migrations and nomad incursions, in Greece, Egypt, Palestine and the Indus Valley. Until now, the connection between chronic drought and unstable social conditions had not been extended to Mesopotamia, the land between the two rivers, the Euphrates and the Tigris, often called "the cradle of civilization."

As to what caused such a persistent dry spell, the scientists said they had no clear ideas, though they suggested that changing wind patterns and ocean currents could have been factors. A tremendous volcanic eruption that occurred in Turkey near the beginning of the drought, the scientists said, almost certainly could not have triggered such a long climate change.

"This is a research frontier for climatologists," Dr. Weiss said in an interview.

Dr. Weiss proposed the new theory for the Akkadian collapse at a recent meeting of the Society of American Archeology in St. Louis and then in a report in the journal *Science*. His principal collaborators in the research were Dr. Marie-Agnes Courty, an archeologist and soil scientist at the National Center for Scientific Research in Paris, and Dr. Francois Guichard, a geologist at the same institution.

Other archeologists said the theory was plausible and appeared to provide the first logical explanation for the Akkadian downfall. Although he had not studied the report, Dr. Robert Biggs, a specialist in Mesopotamian archeology at the University of Chicago, said this was a good example of "archeology's growing sophistication in seeking reasons for serious political changes in the past."

In an article accompanying the report in *Science*, Dr. Robert McC. Adams, secretary of the Smithsonian Institution and an anthropologist specializing in Mesopotamia, cautioned that Dr. Weiss and his colleagues had not thoroughly established the link between climate and the empire's fall. He questioned whether such widespread and persistent drought could be inferred from local soil conditions at a few sites.

"It will demand of other people in the field to either refute it or replicate it with their own work," Dr. Adams said of the theory. "And the only way to get people to pick up that challenge is for Weiss to stick his neck out. I applaud it."

Dr. Weiss said the conclusions were based on tests of soils mainly at the sites of three Akkadian cities within a 30-mile radius, places now known as Tell Leilan, Tell Mozan and Tell Brak in present-day Syria. Evidence of similar climate change was found in adjacent regions, and the archeologist said further tests of the theory would be conducted.

The most revealing evidence has come from Tell Leilan, where Dr. Weiss has been excavating for 14 years and finding successive layers of ruins going back some 8,000 years. For several millennia, this was a small village established by some of the world's first farmers. Around 2600 B.C., it suddenly expanded sixfold to become the city of Shekhna, with 10,000 to 20,000 inhabitants. They lived in the middle of a land of rainy winters, dry summers and a long growing season for wheat and barley, much as it is today.

All the more reason the kings of Akkad, or Agade, a city-state whose location has never been exactly determined but is assumed to have been near ancient Kish and Babylon, reached out and conquered places like Tell Leilan about 2300 B.C. The region became the breadbasket for the Akkadian Empire, which stretched 800 miles from the Persian Gulf to the headwaters of the Euphrates in Turkey.

Ceramics and other artifacts established the Akkadian presence there in Tell Leilan and other northern towns. And for years archeologists puzzled over the 300-year gap in human occupation of Tell Leilan and neighboring towns, beginning in 2200 B.C. It occurred to Dr. Weiss that since no irrigation works had been uncovered there, the region must have relied on rain-fed agriculture, as is the case there today, in contrast to the irrigated farming in southern Mesopotamia. A severe drought, therefore, could be disastrous to life in the north.

This idea was tested by Dr. Courty, using microscopic techniques she pioneered in a scientific specialty, soil micromorphology. By examining in detail the arrangement and nature of sediments at archeological sites, it is possible to reconstruct ancient environmental conditions and human activity.

One of the first discoveries was a half-inch layer of volcanic ash covering the rooftops of buildings at Tell Leilan in 2200 B.C. All ashfalls leave distinctive chemical signatures. An analysis by Dr. Guichard traced the likely source of this potassium-rich ash to volcanoes a few hundred miles away in present-day Turkey.

Since the abandonment of Tell Leilan occurred at the same time and the climate suddenly became more arid, volcanic fallout was first suspected as the culprit. Ash and gases from volcanic eruptions can remain suspended in the atmosphere for years, creating sun-blocking hazes and reducing temperatures. But from their knowledge of recent volcanoes, scientists doubted that the eruptions could have perturbed the climate over such a large area for 300 years.

And there seemed no doubt about the drought lasting that long, Dr. Courty said. In the surrounding countryside at Tell Leilan and elsewhere, she examined a layer of soil nearly two feet thick and lying just above the volcanic ash. This layer contained large amounts of fine wind-blown sand and dust, in contrast to the richer soil in earlier periods. Another telltale sign was the absence of earthworm holes and insect tracks, which are usually present in soils from moister environments.

This was strong evidence, the researchers reported, of a "marked aridity induced by intensification of wind circulation and an apparent increase" of dust storms in the northern plains of Mesopotamia.

It was during the 300-year desertification that archives of the southern cities reported the migration of barbarians from the north and a sharp decline in agricultural production, and showed an increasing number of names of people from the northern tribes, mainly the Amorites.

According to the evidence of the sediments, rain in more abundance returned to northern Mesopotamia in 1900 B.C. and with it the tracks of earthworms and the rebuilding of the deserted cities. Over the ruins of Shekhna, buried in the sands of the drought, rose a new city named Shubat Enlil, which means "dwelling place of Enlil," the paramount Mesopotamian god. The builders were Amorites.

In earlier excavations at Tell Leilan, Dr. Weiss discovered an archive of clay tablets showing that this was the lost capital of a northern Amorite kingdom often mentioned in the cuneiform writing of the period. This was the archive of Shamshi-Adad, the Amorite king who reigned from 1813 to 1781 B.C., containing the king's correspondence with neighboring rulers who concluded the ransoming of spies.

By then, the Akkadian kingdom of Sargon and Naram-Sin—the world's first empire—was long lost in the dust, apparently also the first empire to collapse as a result of catastrophic climate change.

"Since this is probably the first abrupt climate change in recorded history that caused major social upheaval," Dr. Weiss said, "it raises some interesting questions about how volatile climate conditions can be and how well civilizations can adapt to abrupt crop failures."

—JOHN NOBLE WILFORD, August 1993

FROM THE AKKADIANS TO BABYLON

- Sometime before the third millennium B.C.: a tribe of Semitic-speaking herding nomads, perhaps orginally from Arabia, gradually settles down in northern Mesopotamia, which comes to be called Akkad.
- Middle of the third millennium B.C.: Akkadian names first appear in Sumerian documents.
- Around 2500 B.C.: inscriptions written in Akkadian appear.
- 2340–2316 B.C.: reign of Lugal-zagesi, last of a line of Sumerian kings. It is a time of struggles among city-states for regional supremacy.
- Around 2300 B.C.: rise of Sargon of Agade or Akkad, a Semitic-speaking ruler; he defeats Lugal-zagesi and reigns for 56 years. The exact location of his city has never been found.
- 2278–2270 B.C.: reign of his son Rimush, killed in a palace revolt.
- 2270–2254 B.C.: reign of Rimush's brother Manishtushu, also killed in a palace revolt.
- 2254–2218 B.C.: reign of Manishtushu's son Naram-Sin, thought to be the first to claim kingship as a divine right. His downfall was traditionally ascribed to divine retribution in the form of invading hordes from the east, called the Gutians. However, new research suggests complex internal problems and the beginning of a 300-year drought as the culprits.
- 2217–2193 B.C.: reign of his son Shar-kali-sharri, followed by a period of anarchy.

- 2200 B.C.: volcanic eruption in Anatolia, after which many Akkadian settlements are abandoned.
- Around 2220–2120 B.C.: a Gutian dynasty is recorded, among others.
- 2123–2113 B.C.: rise of Utu-hegal, who appoints Ur-Nammu as military governor at Ur. Ur-Nammu overthrows his protector, assumes the title of King of Ur and founds a well-organized dynasty. The ziggurat, or stepped tower, prototype of the Tower of Babel, is first recorded in his reign. Ur falls gradually, besieged by invaders like the Amorites and Elamites.
- 2028–2004 B.C.: reign of Ibbi-Sin ends with loss of empire. Some years later, a former underling, Ishbi-Erra, expels the Elamites.
- 1984–1975 B.C.: his son, Shu-ilishu, using the title King of Ur, continues a dynasty noted for peace and prosperity. Amorite influence remains strong and the desert sheiks who lead them are respected. An Amorite dynasty is founded at Larsa. Amorites are gradually assimilated into the Babylonian population.
- 1932–1906 B.C.: an Amorite king, Gungunum, claims titles of King of Sumer and Akkad and of Ur.
- Around 1894 B.C.: emergence of an Amorite dynasty at Babylon. A city called Shubat-Enlil is built on the ruins of Shekhna, abandoned in the drought.
- 1813–1781 B.C.: reign of Shamshi-Adad, a powerful Amorite king.
- 1792–1750 B.C.: reign of Hammurabi, famous king and lawgiver; toward the end of his reign, Babylon becomes a great military power and the seat of kingship.
- 1595 B.C.: sack of Babylon by the Hittites, an Indo-European-speaking people from Asia Minor.

6

DOOMSDAY FROM SPACE

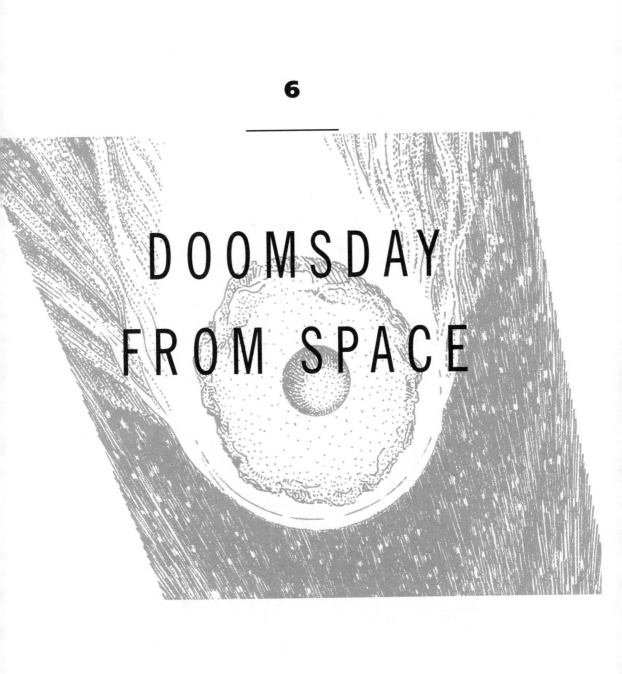

n the course of the 1990s, what began as a far-out idea has ended as conventional wisdom. The Earth is not an isolated blue haven in the voids of space, but is subject to the violent forces that rule the evolution of planetary systems. Every few tens of millions of years, a comet or asteroid will crash into the planet's surface, liberating titanic blasts of heat and rock dust and changing the planet's face for ever.

For years geologists were unwilling to accept this theory, not so much because of its alarming implications but because they were schooled in the doctrine of uniformitarianism—that slow, steady changes from within the Earth provide the best explanations of all its surface features.

Now that the reality of periodic asteroid strikes is well accepted, attention has turned to assessing the likelihood of future strikes. Astronomers are using special telescopes to catalog all the Earth-crossing asteroids—those whose orbits cross the Earth's path around the sun. So far some 200 Earth-crossers have been found and experts expect up to 4,000 may exist.

Once the asteroids have been cataloged, their orbits can be predicted and estimates made of the likely date of any future collision with Earth. So far none has been found to present any imminent threat. Should one turn up, there would probably be years if not decades in which to consider appropriate countermeasures.

Far less predictable is the hazard from comets. These balls of rock and ice inhabit belts at the very edges of the solar system, beyond the view of telescopes, and no rhyme or reason has yet been discerned in the pattern of their visitations. The spectacular eruptions caused in July 1994 when the comet Shoemaker-Levy crashed into the face of Jupiter underscored the destructiveness of any comet that might collide with Earth.

Even assuming that our descendants learn successfully how to defend Earth from comets and asteroids, the sun, like any star, has a finite lifetime. Astronomers believe it will die in a fiery series of explosions that will blow off most of its outer layers. Well before then it will have ballooned into a red giant, either engulfing the Earth or heating it to searing temperatures.

The soonest this unpleasant event could occur is in one billion years from now. Perhaps that is time enough to evade the catastrophe. On the other hand, if life on Earth started 3.5 to 4 billion years ago, then more than 70 percent of the planet's inhabitable lifetime is over.

Asteroid Defense: "Risk Is Real," Planners Say

TOO FAINT TO BE SEEN by the naked eye, the first asteroid was discovered in 1801 by an Italian monk named Guiseppi Piazzi, working at an observatory in Palermo, Sicily. By the end of the century, astronomers armed with more powerful telescopes were tracking hundreds of these rocky bodies, which lie in a loose belt between Mars and Jupiter like so much rubble left over from creation.

A troubling new kind of asteroid was found in 1932, one whose eccentric orbit occasionally brings it hurtling across the path of the Earth. But astronomers did not start looking systematically for Earth-crossing asteroids until quite recently, their search spurred by the theory that periodic asteroid impacts, tens of millions of years apart, have shaped the evolution of life.

Today, the total number of Earth-crossing asteroids stands at about 150, with two or three more being discovered each month. The largest found so far is about five miles wide. With computers, scientists have predicted the paths of such objects well into the twenty-first century. No known asteroid is expected to hit the Earth in that time.

The issue of whether mankind should worry about asteroids recently got a new level of official recognition as a government-appointed team suggested a $50 million plan for an early warning system. Critics were quick to denounce it as make-work for astronomers and for weapon makers eager for a new threat after the Cold War. But the authors insist that their report draws on a wealth of evidence that astronomers, geologists and biologists have accumulated over the last decade.

The large team of scientists organized by the National Aeronautics and Space Administration, responding to a request from the House Sci-

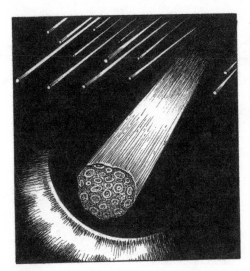

The Earth is occasionally hit by craggy remnants of creation known as asteroids. About 150 are known to cross the Earth's path. There may be as many as 4,200 Earth-crossers big enough to cause global effects if they hit. Astronomers want to find and track them to avert the threat.

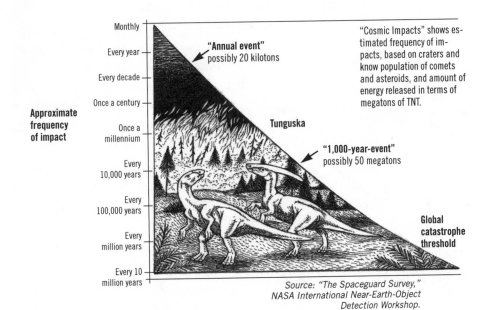

"Annual event" possibly 20 kilotons

Tunguska

"1,000-year-event" possibly 50 megatons

"Cosmic Impacts" shows estimated frequency of impacts, based on craters and know population of comets and asteroids, and amount of energy released in terms of megatons of TNT.

Approximate frequency of impact

Monthly
Every year
Every decade
Once a century
Once a millennium
Every 10,000 years
Every 100,000 years
Every million years
Every 10 million years

Global catastrophe threshold

Source: "The Spaceguard Survey,"
NASA International Near-Earth-Object
Detection Workshop.

ence Committee, laid out a plan for creating the first complete census of the menacing rocks. Six ground-based telescopes would be built around the globe to scan the heavens and provide warning of impending danger, often decades in advance of its approach and in time enough for work to begin on interceptors to deflect the asteroid. The team put the cost of the telescopes at $50 million plus $10 million a year for their operation. It recommended international financing because the benefits would be global.

In the report, the team estimated that, all told, the telescopes might find 1,050 to 4,200 Earth-crossing asteroids that are at least 0.62 miles in diameter, a size judged large enough to begin to cause global upheaval by deranging climate and agriculture. Even quite small rocks are of possible concern since their enormous speeds endow them with kinetic energy that is converted at impact into quantities of heat comparable to that released by multiple nuclear explosions.

Slamming into the Earth at roughly 16 miles a second, a large asteroid could explode with the force of a million H-bombs, lofting enough pulverized rock and dust to block most sunlight. Cold and darkness could last for months, crippling agriculture and probably a good part of modern civilization, leading to the deaths of a billion or more people from starvation.

"The risk is real," Dr. David Morrison of NASA's Ames Research Center in California, who was cochairman of the study by nearly 100 scientists, said in an interview.

Skeptics disagree, dismissing the asteroid hazard as ridiculously small and belittling the NASA team as either laughably paranoid or, worse yet, conspiring for a lifetime of entitlements for astronomers and would-be makers of interceptors. What could be more suspicious, cynics ask, than astronomers offering to save the Earth from a cosmic disaster with just a few new telescopes?

In an editorial, *The Washington Times* scorned the NASA team's plan as a "scam to make away with taxpayers' money," adding that "there's no evidence that anyone in all of human history has ever been killed by an asteroid."

Members of the team, who come from places like Cornell University, the Lowell Observatory, the University of Arizona and the California Institute of Technology, tend to take such criticism in stride.

"We looked at this in the most careful, reasoned way we could," said Dr. Richard P. Binzel, an asteroid expert at the Massachusetts Institute of Technology. "Although the threat is small, it's not zero. There's probably a one-in-seven thousand chance that an impact with global repercussions could happen in a person's lifetime. If you want to gamble with that level of risk, that's okay. It's really a political decision as to whether the threat is judged big enough to warrant investing in some insurance."

Dr. Morrison takes the critical jabs philosophically, saying the asteroid threat has dawned on scientists only slowly and is hard for laymen to comprehend. But the unambiguous fact, he said, is that mankind lives in a kind of cosmic shooting gallery.

"This does not fall within our ordinary experience, so it takes some getting used to," he said in an interview.

Evidence of the danger, as outlined in the NASA report and interviews with major authors, is extensive, if at times circumstantial. One clue, Dr. Morrison said, is the large number of impact craters found throughout the solar system by robot spacecraft exploring planets. Moreover, he said, geologists have only begun to realize in the past two decades that numerous craters exist on Earth. Some 130 have been discovered, with the list growing by five or six a year. The largest crater, which is in Ontario, is 124 miles from rim to rim.

For centuries the Earth craters were either not recognized or thought to be of volcanic origin. If the craters had not been eroded by the Earth's atmosphere and oceans, they would be as prominent as those on the Moon.

New awareness of asteroid impacts has increased the appreciation of close encounters and mysterious events. In 1908 in the Tunguska region of Siberia, a cosmic object that never reached the Earth's surface exploded in the atmosphere with a force of some 20 H-bombs, the resulting shock wave flattening hundreds of square miles of forest. Scientists now calculate the object was perhaps a mere 150 feet in diameter.

Another line of evidence in the NASA report comes from the fossil record and ancient stone. In 1980, Luis W. Alvarez, a Nobel laureate at the University of California, and others proposed that 65 million years ago an asteroid impact and its global pall of dust resulted in the mass extinction of many life forms, including the dinosaurs. Although the Alvarez hypothesis is still much debated, its supporters have gathered much geological evidence to buttress the idea. Today many scientists think that a huge asteroid, perhaps 10 miles wide, slammed into the Caribbean basin near Mexico to wipe out some 60 percent of all Earth's life-forms.

Indeed, one school of biologists now believes that asteroids over the eons have periodically ended the rule of dominant species, encouraging new forms of life to take over ecological niches and shaping the evolution of life on Earth.

A further type of evidence is the ease with which a handful of observers, led by Dr. Eugene M. Shoemaker, a geologist-turned-astronomer from the United States Geological Survey, have found Earth-crossing asteroids. Relatively small efforts have produced large numbers of discoveries.

Today, the most up-to-date search is led by Dr. Tom Gehrels, a professor of lunar and planetary science at the University of Arizona. Since the late 1980s, his 36-inch telescope on Kitt Peak has scanned the sky with an advanced electronic detector, revealing swarms of small asteroids zipping past the Earth at uncomfortably close distances.

On January 18, 1991, his team spotted an asteroid about 30 feet in diameter passing between the Earth and the moon. If it had struck, its enormous velocity would have given the impact the force of several atomic bombs like the one used at Hiroshima.

Dr. Morrison of NASA said the orbits of Earth-crossing asteroids change slowly in relation to the Earth, insuring that a threatening asteroid would typically make hundreds of moderately close passes before colliding. That is good news for advance warning. But over the eons, he noted, such shifts mean that the vast majority of these asteroids will eventually hit the moon or one of the inner planets—Mercury, Venus, Earth or Mars—or will be flung from the inner solar system after a close encounter with a planet.

If a large asteroid crashed into the Earth, the NASA team wrote, the results would range from bad to worse. For asteroids at least 0.62 miles wide or larger, "the greatest hazard derives from the global veil of dust injected into the stratosphere," the report said. "At some size, an impact would lead to massive worldwide crop failures and consequent mass mortality, and would threaten the survival of civilization. At still larger sizes, even the survival of the human species would be put at risk."

What is the risk of a major collision anytime soon? The NASA team found it to be slim but not negligible.

Based on statistics on searches and craters, the team estimated that Earth-threatening asteroids total 1,050 to 4,200. These would be at least

---

Destructive Power Rises with Asteroid Size

Smaller than 33 feet
Tiny asteroid fragments as small as a pea sparkle harmlessly in the night sky as they burn up in the atmosphere, where they are known as meteors. Even asteroids many feet wide often burn up and leave no crater on the Earth's surface, though they can, and frequently do, explode high in the atmosphere.

33 feet to 328 feet
Asteroids of this size, which arrive on a time scale of decades to centuries, produce fireballs equal in power to many nuclear explosions as they explode in the atmosphere, radiating powerful shock waves that can be heard and felt on the ground.

A 200-foot intruder:
A celestial wanderer in 1908 exploded about five miles above the Earth's surface over the desolate region of Tunguska, Siberia, releasing energy equal to about 20 large hydrogen bombs. Trees were flattened over an area larger than New York City and fires were ignited for many miles around by the intense burst of radiant energy.

328 feet to 3,280 feet, or 0.62 miles
Asteroids of this size arrive on a time scale of thousands of years and can survive atmospheric burning to strike Earth and form a crater, ejecting dust and nitric acid into the atmosphere. The map shows the approximately 130 identified impact craters.

0.62 miles and larger
Asteroids of this size are believed able to disrupt life on Earth because of the large amount of dust they throw into the atmosphere, changing the climate for years, maybe decades. They are estimated to strike landmasses once every 300,000 years or so. The severity of the global effects increases with the asteroid's size, and in the modern world would at some point lead to widespread crop failures and starvation.

6.21 miles to 9.31 miles
About 65 million years ago, an asteroid of this size is believed by many scientists to have slammed into the Caribbean basin near present-day Mexico. It is the leading candidate for the asteroid presumed to have killed off the dinosaurs and 60 percent of all the Earth's life-forms at that time.

0.62 miles in diameter, which is considered to be the minimum size for a collision to have global repercussions. Trying to be conservative, the team in its risk estimates trained its sights on Earth-crossing asteroids twice that size, 1.24 miles wide or bigger, of which there are probably far fewer, perhaps 400. The team judged that one might collide with the Earth every 500,000 years, making the annual probability of collision 1 in 500,000.

For a person living for 70 years, Dr. Binzel of M.I.T. said in an interview, the 500,000-year figure means that an individual has about a 1 in 7,000 chance of seeing the Earth in upheaval. Although plane crashes are commonplace by comparison, an individual's lifetime risk of death from an airplane crash is said to be about 1 in 20,000. The lifetime risk of death in an automobile accident is 1 in 100.

"The asteroid risk is small compared to what people are accustomed to, but it's not insignificant," Dr. Binzel said.

As the NASA report put it, "during our lifetime there is a small but nonzero chance (very roughly one in ten thousand) that the Earth will be struck by an object large enough to destroy food crops on a global scale and possibly end civilization as we know it."

In interviews, team members were quick to caution that all their estimates were extremely rough and to suggest that the best way to get a better grip on the problem was to begin a serious survey.

The team said some improvements could be made without building new telescopes. By simply improving equipment at the major existing sites for asteroid watching, the current rate of discovery of Earth-crossing asteroids could probably be doubled. This would cost perhaps $1 million in capital outlays and $1 million a year for operations, the team wrote.

Pinning down the full dimensions of the danger and finding perhaps 90 percent of all Earth-threatening asteroids would require the construction of six new telescopes, the NASA team said. The search would take a quarter century. Such a survey would discover some 500 new Earth-crossing objects each month, the team said, and greatly reduce the chance of an unexpected encounter with a rocky visitor from outer space.

"The survey," the team wrote, "has the potential to alter fundamentally the way we view the threat of cosmic impacts. To date we have talked about a relatively undefined threat, to be discussed in terms of probabilities or statistical risks. While we know such impacts must take place from time to time, we do not know if there are any specific bodies in space that might impact the Earth over the next few centuries."

The team called an expanded survey "a modest investment to provide insurance for our planet against the ultimate catastrophe."

—WILLIAM J. BROAD, April 1992

Scientists Ponder Saving Planet From Earth-Bound Comet

THEORETICIANS OF DOOM, WHO HAVE long pondered the odds of cosmic bombardment and whether a way might be found to save the planet from destruction, always dabbling in abstractions, suddenly have a real case study on their hands with the rediscovery of a large comet now calculated to have roughly a 1-in-10,000 chance of hitting Earth.

While low odds of disaster rule out a sense of urgency, as does the distant date of potential collision, August 14, 2126, doomsday scientists are nonetheless having a field day as they envision ways to track and divert the icy interloper, cheerily hoping against hope that they can ride to the rescue with their rockets and nuclear warheads.

They calculate that, in theory, there are three main opportunities for emergency action before the possible crackup of comet and planet: 134 years, 4 years and 15 days before collision. The longer the period of inaction, these experts say, the bigger the effort needed to deflect the speeding intruder. A last-minute diversion would require a giant nuclear explosion some 100,000 times larger than the blast that leveled Hiroshima.

The comet, a mountain of ice and dirt some six miles in diameter, is now hurtling through the inner solar system at 37 miles a second. On its return 134 years from now, it has a remote chance of striking Earth.

Its speed and size are judged to be large enough so that its impact would be similar to many thousands of nuclear warheads going off simultaneously on the same spot, creating a global pall of dust that would block sunlight, disrupt the climate and possibly end civilization. Such a collision 65 million years ago is widely believed to have contributed to the extinction of the dinosaurs.

Eager to avoid that kind of predicament, and apparently happy to try on the role of planetary saviors, federal and private scientists are now quietly working computers, faxes and telephone lines, calculating how, when and where a nudge or two from a nuclear weapon or a futuristic reactor might divert Swift-Tuttle from a doomsday course.

"We could definitely deal with it," Dr. John D. G. Rather, assistant director for space technology at the National Aeronautics and Space Administration, who led a recent federal study on cosmic interdiction, said in an interview.

"It's a facinating topic," said Dr. Jondale C. Solem, a physicist at the Los Alamos National Laboratory in New Mexico who aided the study. "These things are going to hammer our planet every one hundred million years or so and produce a massive extinction until a species evolves that can do something about it."

Skeptics say the current interest in Swift-Tuttle is a result of scheming by astronomers and bomb makers to drum up business by practicing the kind of threat inflation the Pentagon excelled at in the Cold War.

But doomsday enthusiastis insist the threat is real, saying space is swarming with thousands of Earth-crossing asteroids and comets that could wreak global havoc and, given enough time, undoubtedly will do so. They note that it was Congress in 1990 that asked the National Aeronautics and Space Administration to conduct a major study of the problem after a half-mile-wide asteroid crossed Earth's path at an uncomfortably close range.

In late March, the large NASA team that conducted the study made headlines by calling for an international effort to scan the heavens for impending danger, saying an organized effort would "provide insurance for our planet."

The study's leaders now say that in all probability during the twenty-second century Swift-Tuttle will not be the beginning of the end. But they insist that the comet, at the very least, should now be tracked closely to better understand its orbit and to refine the odds of disaster.

"One in ten thousand is not an infinitesimal risk," said Dr. Clark R. Chapman, an astronomer at the Planetary Science Institute in Tucson, Arizona, a private group. If the comet turns out to be a serious threat, he added, "our great-great-grandchildren would have to deal with it, not ourselves."

The comet got its name during the Civil War when it was sighted July 16, 1862, by an American astronomer, Lewis Swift, in upstate New York and independently three days later by another astronomer, Horace Tuttle, at Harvard University. It brightened in September into an object visible to the naked eye, which became known as the Great Comet of 1862.

Today astronomers believe Swift-Tuttle causes the annual Perseid meteor shower, which usually peaks in August. The comet's repeated passes through the solar system over the ages, all the while shedding bits of dust and debris, have formed a river of particles along its path. As Earth passes through this river each year, the sky comes alive with flashes of light. The Perseids are the best known and most reliable of the many meteor showers throughout the year.

Swift-Tuttle's own placement in this well-known orbital band was something of a mystery until late September of 1992 when Tsuruhiko Kiuchi, a Japanese amateur astronomer using a large pair of binoculars, rediscovered it. The sighting was the most important since the reappearance of Halley's comet nearly a decade ago.

Soon after Swift-Tuttle's closest approach to Earth it may become visible to the naked eye. And the following year, astronomers say, the Perseid shower is unusually bright, having been recently recharged by the comet's passage.

The reappearance turned ominous after astronomers used new sightings to predict the comet's future path. And the International Astronomical Union, the world astronomy authority, issued its first warning of a potential collision between Earth and a large object from outer space, saying there was a slight chance Swift-Tuttle might strike Earth on its next pass.

The uncertainty is great because astronomers have no idea how much its orbit will be shifted by the eruptive forces on the comet's surface, which increase as it nears the sun and work like rocket engines.

"We know nongravitational effects are at work," said Dr. Brian G. Marsden of the Harvard-Smithsonian Center for Astrophysics in Cambridge, Massachusetts, "but we don't know to what extent."

Dr. Marsden, who wrote the union's warning, has encouraged the group's members to train telescopes on the comet to better understand its orbit, especially after it has left the sun's vicinity in a few years and the jet-like activity has stopped.

Some scientists cast doubt Dr. Marsden's current 1-in-10,000 estimate for the risk of the comet's hitting Earth, saying the odds of collision may be far lower. "There's some tiny chance the thing would hit us," said Dr. Alan W. Harris, a planetary scientist at NASA's Jet Propulsion Laboratory in Pasadena, California.

But Dr. Harris also cautioned that the exact extent of risk could long remain a mystery since forecasts could be rendered obsolete by unrecognized gravitational forces working on the comet in the icy fringes of the solar system, beyond the ken of Earth's observatories.

"It could be subject to major perturbations in the outer planets," Dr. Harris said. "It's hard to make predictions that hold up for a hundred and thirty-four years."

A much easier job, he said, is tracking Earth-crossing asteroids, rocky bodies that circle the sun every few years and sometimes pass through Earth's path. The larger of these are often able to be observed continually.

Given the limitations of comet watching and predicting, some students of the doomsday collision, like Dr. Gregory H. Canavan of the Los Alamos laboratory, have informally proposed that a radio beacon be attached to Swift-Tuttle so its progress through the solar system can be more easily monitored. But others say it is already too late for such a rendezvous. They point out that the comet will soon be moving rapidly away from Earth and would be very difficult for a rocket to overtake.

The ease or difficulty of diverting a comet, experts say, depends on how much time scientists have to prepare. If decades or centuries are available, an orbit in theory could be shifted by placing a nuclear or chemical reactor on the comet's surface that would very slowly turn ice into jets of steam firing like small rockets, similar to natural volatility. Even a relatively small force, applied at an early stage, could significantly shift a comet's orbit since the small changes would add up dramatically over great distances.

But even if the comet were judged a serious threat today, while still in Earth's vicinity, there would be little or no time to develop and field the complex equipment needed for such a leisurely approach. Thus, the first plausible opportunity for a rendezvous would be out past Saturn on its return in the twenty-second century as the comet moved through the plane of the planets. That would be about four years before a possible collision with Earth.

Dr. Solem of Los Alamos has calculated that at that point a nuclear explosion equal to 10 million tons of high explosive would be needed to nudge the comet's orbit enough so it would just miss Earth. To be prudent, he said, the nuclear explosion should probably be on the order of 100 million tons, and backup bombs should be ready for action.

America's first hydrogen bomb, exploded in 1952, had a force of about 10 million tons of high explosive and was about 700 times more powerful than the atomic bomb dropped on Hiroshima. The largest nuclear blast of all time, achieved by the Russians, had a force equal to about 60 million tons of high explosive.

If an armada of nuclear-tipped interceptors failed to divert the comet beyond Saturn, another opportunity would occur in the year 2126 during its closest approach to the sun, some 15 days before slamming into Earth. At that point, to produce the same degree of diversion, Dr. Solem said, a nuclear explosion would have to be about 100 times larger, equal to billions of tons of high explosive.

A cometary near miss, Dr. Solem noted, "would still be a spectacular sight" as the giant fireball of Swift-Tuttle blazed through Earth's outer atmosphere, lighting the sky in a brilliant display of fireworks that would last about three minutes.

If all attempts at diversion failed, and the comet and Earth collide on August 14, 2126, during the exceedingly small window of vulnerability that day, which is only three or four minutes long, the results by all accounts would be horrific.

Asteroids move along at roughly 16 or 17 miles a second in relation to Earth, while Swift-Tuttle would be zipping along at more than twice that speed, 37 miles a second, increasing its energy of collision nearly sixfold over that of an asteroid.

Earth's atmosphere would offer no resistance, being essentially invisible to the speeding comet.

As the comet struck ocean or dry land, vaporizing on contact, heaving boulders into the sky, pulverizing rocks and sending clouds of dust around the globe, the explosion would be larger than the one that is thought to have helped wipe out the dinosaurs.

"This would finish us off," Dr. Solem remarked. "Whether you're in New York or Afghanistan or wherever, the impact would be global. I don't think *Homo sapiens* would survive."

—WILLIAM J. BROAD, November 1992

NASA Photographs an Asteroid Giving Earth a Close Shave, Sort of

THE FIRST CLOSE-UP PHOTOGRAPH of a speeding asteroid whose path in space crosses Earth's orbit, raising the possibility of a fiery collision on some far-off day, was the image of the four-mile-long asteroid, named Toutatis, made by ground-based radar as it zipped past Earth at a distance of 2.2 million miles, a near miss by celestial standards.

Over the years astronomers have found more than 150 rocky asteroids whose eccentric orbits occasionally bring them hurtling across the path of the Earth, and they believe space is swarming with thousands more. Until now, these Earth-crossing asteroids have generally been seen only as distant points of light, even in powerful telescopes.

Now, using a new radar system at NASA's deep-space tracking station in the Mojave Desert, a team of astronomers at the Jet Propulsion Laboratory in Pasadena, California, has obtained several images of Toutatis, revealing a surprisingly jagged shape indicative of a cataclysmic past.

"This is our first clear look at one of the many thousands of asteroids whose orbits can intersect the Earth's," said Dr. Steven Ostro, a senior research scientist at the laboratory and leader of the radar team.

Most asteroids lie in a loose belt between Mars and Jupiter, like so much rubble left over from creation. Indeed, some scientists speculate that that is just what they are.

Toutatis (pronounced too-TAT-is) was discovered by French astronomers in 1990, and was named after the Gallic god of tribal protection. Almost nothing of its nature was known until now.

The NASA radar images reveal it to consist of two craggy, heavily cratered objects about 1.6 miles and 2.5 miles in diameter.

"The binary nature of Toutatis is the most important single result of this radar experiment," said Dr. Ostro, noting that earlier, more primitive radar studies of asteroids had only hinted at the possibility of dumbbell shapes.

"It's the most complex shape we've seen in the solar system," he said in an interview. "It's a wonderful, extraordinary object."

He speculated that Toutatis might be the residue of a much larger body in the main asteroid belt that was fractured and cast asunder in a collision with another large object. The pieces that make up Toutatis's "contact binary" form, he added, might have merged in a relatively gentle crackup.

Another possibility, he said, was that Toutatis was split by a collision not quite powerful enough to send the pieces flying off in different directions, their mutual gravitational attraction keeping them in proximity.

The radar observations were carried out at NASA's Goldstone Deep Space Communications Complex in the Mojave Desert. In its closest approach to the Earth, Toutatis was about 10 times the distance from the Earth to the moon.

For most of the radar study, Goldstone's main 230-foot dish antenna directed a 400,000-watt beam of radio energy at the asteroid. The signals, which took as little as 24 seconds to speed to and from Toutatis, were received by Goldstone's new 112-foot antenna, and were thereafter subjected to advanced processing to tease from them as much information as possible.

"The image is a hundred times better than any other of a small celestial body that's been achieved with Earth-based radar," said Dr. Ostro, adding that image processing of the Toutatis data in the next few months is expected to reveal features as small as 330 feet across.

In addition to Dr. Ostro, members of the radar team are Dr. Raymond Jurgens, Keith Rosema, Ron Winkler, Denise Howard, Randy Rose, Dr. Martin Slade and Dr. Donald Yeomans.

The only other close-up picture of an asteroid was taken in 1991 by the NASA probe Galileo bound for Jupiter. Its subject, Gaspra, was also revealed to be a lumpy body bearing the scars of a turbulent history. The photograph session occurred while Galileo and Gaspra were some 10,000 miles apart. Gaspra's orbit does not cross the Earth's.

The only close-up pictures of a comet are those of Halley, taken by a European robot probe in 1986.

Although potential killer comets and asteroids have lately been in the news, astronomers recently gave Earth a reprieve from Comet Swift-Tuttle, deciding that previous predictions of its having a slight chance of collision with the Earth in 2126 were incorrect.

In an interview, Dr. Ostro said that in general the threat of doomsday from space had been exaggerated.

"There's all kinds of good reasons to study these things without re-sorting to hand waving," he said. "They're little worlds that have histories of their own that can tell us a lot about the evolution of the solar system."

—WILLIAM J. BROAD, January 1993

Meteoroids Hit Atmosphere in Atomic-Size Blasts

SECRET data from military satellites in orbit thousands of miles above Earth show that the planet is continually bombarded by big meteoroids that explode in blasts the size of atomic detonations. The data, from spacecraft meant to watch for rocket firings and nuclear explosions, were declassified recently by the Defense Department.

From 1975 to 1992, the satellites detected 136 explosions high in the atmosphere, an average of eight a year. The blasts are calculated to have intensities roughly equal to 500 to 15,000 tons of high explosive, or the power of small atomic bombs. Experts who have analyzed the data are publishing it in the book *Hazards Due to Comets and Asteroids* (University of Arizona Press). They say that the detection rate is probably low and that the actual bombardment rate might be 10 times higher, with 80 or so blasts occurring each year.

The disclosure of a new class of large meteoric impacts is seen as bolstering the idea that Earth is subjected to strikes from space in a wide range of severities, including an occasional doomsday rock perhaps once every 10 million years or so that causes mayhem and death on a planetary scale.

The new data are also being praised as a Cold War spinoff that can aid the cause of world peace by preventing false warnings of nuclear attack. Indeed, it turns out that federal analysts on several occasions have struggled quietly for months to determine if such explosions were natural or manmade.

Finally, impact specialists hope the release of formerly secret data will be repeated and promote a new alliance between astronomers and the keepers of military reconnaissance.

"It's important," Dr. Eugene M. Shoemaker, an astronomer at the Lowell Observatory in Flagstaff, Arizona, who helped found the field of Earth-impact studies, said of the new data in an interview. "It's a unique source of scientific information."

Sky and Telescope magazine, based in Cambridge, Massachusetts, lauded the once-secret sightings as "an unprecedented body of spaceborne observations."

Sighted for ages but understood in detail only recently, meteoroids are rubble left over from the creation of the solar system. They are composed of ice, rock, iron and nickel in a variety of shapes and sizes.

Meteor showers and individual streaks of light that flash across the sky every night are generated when tiny flecks of celestial detritus, often no larger than grains of sand or pebbles, burn up while speeding through the atmosphere.

In contrast, the blasts seen by the military satellites are produced when speeding objects up to the size of large houses are heated to incandescence and then explode about 17 to 20 miles above Earth. They create vast fireballs and powerful shock waves that nonetheless leave few or no discernible traces on the ground, since they begin so high up. If made of dense metal, meteoroids of this size have a good chance of punching through the atmosphere to hit the ground.

In general, the new observations are of a class of meteoroids too big to burn up harmlessly in the sky as shooting stars but too small to slice through Earth's atmosphere and strike the ground. They are middle children in the meteoroid family.

By definition, meteoroids are small bodies speeding through space that strike Earth's atmosphere. They can be comets made of ice or asteroids made of stone or metal. Meteors are streaks of light seen when meteoroids are heated while traveling through the atmosphere. Meteorites are the parts of relatively large meteoroids that survive passage through the atmosphere and fall to Earth as chunks of metal and stone.

The scientists who are publishing the new observations say the explosions of large meteoroids previously went largely unreported for many reasons. The vast majority occurred over the oceans or desolate parts of the continents. Many were obscured by clouds. And even when occurring in broad daylight and rivaling the sun in brightness, the explosions lasted only a second or so, limiting the opportunities for observation.

"There's many more of these objects impacting the Earth than we previously thought," said Dr. Edward Tagliaferri, a physicist who was the lead author of the satellite report. "Their discovery is a fascinating story." Dr. Tagliaferri is a consultant for the Aerospace Corporation, a nonprofit engineering firm in El Segundo, California, that helps the Air Force run its numerous satellites.

Dr. Tom Gehrels heads a small team of astronomers who use a 36-inch telescope on Kitt Peak, west of Tucson, to search the sky for asteroids in orbit around the sun that occasionally intersect Earth's orbit and one day might strike the planet. The effort is known as Spacewatch. Such research has so far identified a total of 185 potential interlopers. Generally these are larger than the objects that set off the satellite-observed explosions. Yet the mere existence of the big ones, and other clues like the heavy cratering on the moon, have long implied that space is filled with swarms of smaller objects, which went largely unreported until now.

"It's a very interesting situation," Dr. Gehrels said in an interview. "Spacewatch is finding a certain number of objects in space that agrees with the things Tagliaferri is finding. The picture is consistent."

From such data, scientists have constructed a curve showing how often meteoroids of a given size might be expected to hit Earth. The curve predicted swarms of mid-size objects in about the numbers now being inferred from the military satellite records. The new data, in turn, support the validity of the curve that predicted them and increase confidence that the other end of the curve can help estimate the frequency of truly catastrophic events.

Dr. Clark R. Chapman, a senior scientist at the Planetary Science Institute, based in Tucson, cautioned that new disclosures and the raw data on which they are based had to be carefully analyzed before their soundness could be ascertained.

"I and most of my colleagues would like to see the data, not just the conclusions," he said. "So far it's more than we've seen before, but I'm not going to give it too much weight until I know more about it."

In the twentieth century, the most celebrated collision between Earth and an object from space occurred in 1908 in the Tunguska region of

Siberia. The object exploded in the atmosphere with a force of some 20 hydrogen bombs, its shock waves flattening hundreds of square miles of forest and registering on scientific instruments around the globe.

Reports of similar encounters over the decades have been rare. A near miss occurred in 1972 when a large asteroid, estimated at up to 260 feet in diameter, or nearly the length of a football field, sped through the upper atmosphere over the northern United States and Canada, blazing across the sky in a daylight fireball witnessed by thousands of people before it reentered space.

Unknown to the public, military satellites in space for decades have been seeing large numbers of atmospheric blasts. The main witnesses have been early-warning craft known as D.S.P., for Defense Support Program, which perch in orbits some 23,300 miles above Earth, their telescopes searching the globe for signs of rocket attack. The sensors are said to mainly work in the infrared part of the electromagnetic spectrum, which is the domain in which heat is registered.

"D.S.P. has been seeing these for a long time and ignoring them," said Dr. Gregory H. Canavan, a physicist at the Los Alamos National Laboratory in New Mexico who works and publishes in the Earth-impact field.

The first effort to collect such data systematically began in 1975, Dr. Tagliaferri said. One motivation was to help the Defense Department distinguish between natural explosions and those caused by humans. The collection process was systematic but informal. Magnetic tapes on which raw data existed were usually recycled, so that the preservation of information depended largely on the skills and interests of individual Defense Support Program watch officers, who scanned the sky for trouble.

The importance of the analytical effort was driven home within the Pentagon bureaucracy in 1979, when a mysterious flash occurred over the Indian Ocean. Its geographical proximity to South Africa raised questions about whether it was a clandestine nuclear test, with the issue being hotly debated for years. Another flash near South Africa in December 1980 prompted another round of debate, with Pentagon analysts concluding two months later that the flash was evidently from a meteor.

The new report on the 136 atmospheric explosions is the first overview of this informational treasure trove. The report identifies no satellite system by name, but says at least two types were involved: an infrared system to search for rocket launchings, and a visible-light system to detect nuclear bursts. The former system is apparently operated by the Air Force and the latter one by the Energy Department.

The coauthors of the chapter in *Hazards Due to Comets and Asteroids,* in addition to Dr. Tagliaferri, are Dr. Richard Spalding and Dr. Cliff Jacobs of the Energy Department's Sandia National Laboratories in Albuquerque, New Mexico, Col. Simon P. Worden of the Air Force and Dr. Adam Erlich of Comprehensive Technologies International in Arlington, Virginia, a military contractor.

Colonel Worden, who also holds a doctorate in astronomy, is credited as being the main force behind the declassification of the secret data.

In an interview, Dr. Tagliaferri said the satellite systems, which he declined to name, were built and operated so they had about a 20 percent chance of seeing the one- or two-second flash of a meteoroid explosion anywhere around the globe. That uncertainty in trying to understand the overall rate of planetary bombardment was compounded, he said, by that fact that recording the data was usually an on-again, off-again affair.

"My sense is that there are about ten times as many events" as were recorded, he said. "But there is no way to know."

He said calculations showed that the 136 blasts ranged from the equivalent of roughly 500 tons of high explosives up to 15,000 tons, the latter amountbeing the force of the nuclear bomb that leveled Hiroshima. The most accurately measured blasts were viewed by multiple satellite sensors. Of these, according to the book chapter, the brightest occurred on April 15, 1988, high above Indonesia. Its power was calculated to be equal to 5,000 tons of high explosives.

An observer on the ground 20 miles away would have seen a flash of light the brightness of the sun, the chapter says. Dr. Tagliaferri added that he knew of no reports of the explosion from Indonesia. It occurred at 11:20 A.M.

Another large explosion viewed by more than one satellite occurred on October 1, 1990, over the Pacific Ocean and had a force larger than 1,000 tons of high explosives. A subsequent analysis concluded that the exploding object had been a stony, 100-ton asteroid.

"The Central Pacific asteroid detonation was originally collected as a potential nuclear event, and it took several months, using the most sophisticated sensors and algorithms available, to determine the detonation's true source," a manuscript of the book chapter states. "This suggests that developing nations and potential combatants worldwide, with considerably less sophisticated equipment, might potentially misidentify one of these detonations as a nuclear attack and 'retaliate' against the country's most likely aggressor."

In an interview, Dr. Tagliaferri noted that some widely reported events have been missed by the military satellites. On October 9, 1992, for instance, a bright streak across the East Coast sky ended in Peekskill, New York, coming to Earth to slam through a 1980 red Chevrolet Malibu. The resulting hole went though the trunk and the gas tank. Found beneath the car was a smoking, football-size rock in a crater six inches deep.

"By accident," Dr. Tagliaferri said, "we didn't get anything on that."

—WILLIAM J. BROAD, January 1994

New Look at Apocalypse: Dying Sun Will Boil Seas and Leave Orbiting Cinder

EVEN SUPPOSING THAT MANKIND ONE day stems the population explosion and finds ways to prevent famines, wars, epidemics, the impacts of asteroids and other global catastrophes, Earth will still confront its ultimate doom: a bloated, searing sun is destined to scorch and melt the planet, wiping it clean of life.

But a new and highly detailed projection of the sun's future behavior suggests that the Earth may escape being swallowed and annihilated by the sun, as some astrophysicists had predicted. The planet will still be melted and purged of life, but it will probably survive as a blob of matter and later as a frozen cinder.

Taking into account the sun's present composition, mass and stage of evolution, a team of scientists has improved the precision of previous forecasts, concluding that the sun will expire in a series of helium flashes that will carry away 40 percent of its mass. They calculate the Earth has a minimum of 1.1 billion years before it becomes uninhabitable, an estimate that does not greatly differ from earlier projections. That would mean that terrestrial life has already used up three quarters of its allotted span, since life originated at least 3.5 billion years ago.

The new analysis was prepared by Dr. I. Juliana Sackman of the California Institute of Technology and Dr. Arnold I. Boothroyd of the Canadian Institute for Theoretical Astrophysics at the University of Toronto, incorporating projections by Dr. James F. Kasting, an atmospheric scientist, and Dr. Kenneth Caldeira, a geochemist, both of Pennsylvania State University. Their study for the first time offers precise estimates of the probable effects of a dying sun on global climate and terrestrial life.

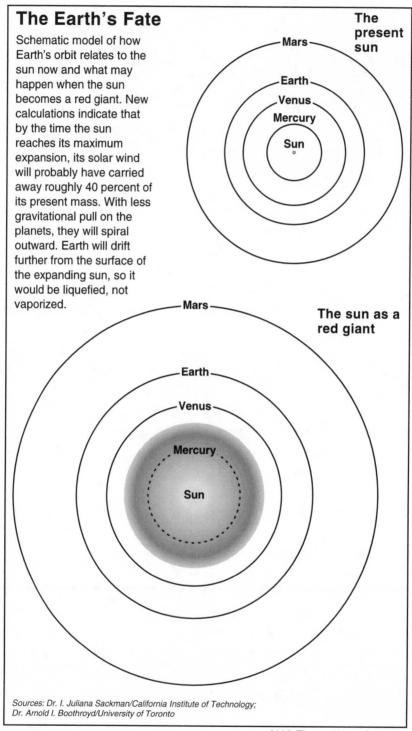

The Earth's Fate

Schematic model of how Earth's orbit relates to the sun now and what may happen when the sun becomes a red giant. New calculations indicate that by the time the sun reaches its maximum expansion, its solar wind will probably have carried away roughly 40 percent of its present mass. With less gravitational pull on the planets, they will spiral outward. Earth will drift further from the surface of the expanding sun, so it would be liquefied, not vaporized.

The present sun

Mars

Earth

Venus

Mercury

Sun

The sun as a red giant

Mars

Earth

Venus

Mercury

Sun

Sources: Dr. I. Juliana Sackman/California Institute of Technology; Dr. Arnold I. Boothroyd/University of Toronto

N.Y. Times News Service

The sun is still certain to evolve into a huge, ultrahot "red giant" that will sterilize Earth as efficiently as a blast furnace. In the report, published in *The Astrophysical Journal,* the scientists used their mathematical model to calculate how much of its mass the sun will lose in the form of solar wind as it undergoes transformation into a red giant, a huge, bright reddish star. Earlier estimates had concluded that in the red giant phase, the sun's width would increase more than 400 times and fill the center of the solar system almost out to Earth's present orbit. The future sun would thus swallow up the planets Mercury and Venus, and possibly Earth.

But Dr. Sackman and her colleagues calculate that by the time the sun reaches its maximum expansion, its solar wind will probably have carried away roughly 40 percent of its present mass.

This means that the sun will exert much less gravitational pull on its planets, all of which will spiral outward. The scientists estimate that Venus will end up 113 million miles from the sun, much farther out than Earth's present distance of 92 million miles from the sun. Earth will drift still farther from the sun, to a distance of 172 million miles.

Dr. Boothroyd cautioned in an interview, however, that there are still many uncertainties about the rate at which the sun will lose mass. This rate will decide whether Earth is engulfed by the sun or merely heated to 2,400 degrees Fahrenheit, at which temperature all its water will have been blasted into space and its surface converted into red-hot molten rock.

No one suggests that people ought to start worrying about the death throes of the sun just yet; the sun has used up only about half of its hydrogen fuel and is still middle-aged.

"All this terrible stuff takes place so far in the future," said Dr. Boothroyd, "that by that time, if the human race survives its own inventions, it could be capable of doing whatever it wanted to survive. It could go some place else."

The new home for the human race might be a planet farther from the sun, or even a planet in another star's system. In principle, he said, future scientists might find a way to shift Earth to a safer orbit farther from the sun. "It's hard to imagine how that could be done, but a billion years is a lot of time," he said. "If we come up with something, it will probably be much sooner than that. Just think how much we've done in the last few hundred years."

Dr. Boothroyd is among the astronomers who believe that travel even between stars may be easier than is now believed, and that some way to "cheat Einstein" by traveling faster than light might one day be discovered.

Dr. Kasting speculated that mankind might find a way to protect Earth from the red-giant sun, postponing global incineration. "A gigantic sun shield might do the trick, at least for a while," he said.

Dr. Edward Teller, who played a pivotal role in the development of the hydrogen bomb, has proposed the use of thermonuclear blasts to divert earthbound asteroids from catastrophic impacts. But he scorns speculative schemes for saving terrestrial life from eventual destruction by the sun.

As the sun heats up and expands, he said, "there will be changes, but these will come after so many other changes that I do not find it terribly interesting to think about it.

"The main point is that probably a significant collision with an asteroid will occur in a couple of hundred years, or, with a smaller probability, a much larger collision," he said. "Therefore it's futile to talk about changes in the very distant future caused by the sun."

The Caltech and Toronto groups are only incidentally interested in the fate of the human race; their main concern is in reconstructing details of the sun's past evolution and future prospects.

Astronomers are confident that their general ideas about the sun's future are correct, because the sun, a G-Class star, belongs to a type that is fairly common. Every stage in the life of this type of star is represented by many examples available in the sky for astronomers to observe and measure.

Early in this century, two astronomers, Ejnar Hertzsprung, a Dane, and Henry Norris Russell, an American, independently discovered a convenient way to group stars according to their types. They found that when the luminosity, or absolute brightness, of a star is compared with its color, the star usually fits into a simple graphic pattern now called the Hertzsprung-Russell Diagram. The pattern is not random. Most stars are restricted to a fairly narrow line on the graph, or to a branch leading away from the line.

When stars are plotted on this diagram according to their luminosity and color, most of them, including the sun, fall on the "main sequence" line, and are believed to evolve in a characteristic way.

With masses about the same as that of the sun, such stars begin their lives when interstellar hydrogen is drawn together by gravitational attraction into a dense cloud. As more and more hydrogen is drawn into such a cloud, it is compressed by gravitational force to high density, high pressure and high temperature. When a protostar becomes sufficiently hot and dense, thermonuclear fusion ignites, hydrogen begins to burn into helium and the star is born, an event that the sun experienced 4.5 billion years ago.

Scientists were astonished to learn several years ago that life began on Earth a geologically short time after the birth of the sun. As early as 3.5 billion years ago, microorganisms were alive in what is now Australia, and the traces they left in sedimentary rock reveal that they had already evolved many different forms early in Earth's infancy.

The sun is a G-Class star because of its luminosity and the color of most of its radiation—visible light centered on the green part of the spectrum, corresponding to a surface temperature of about 6,000 kelvins, or 10,300 degrees Fahrenheit. At present, 4.5 billion years into its "main sequence" phase, the sun is quietly burning its hydrogen supply and increasing very slightly in luminosity. As a G-Class star, it is expected to spend roughly seven billion more years on the main sequence.

But life on Earth will disappear long before the sun leaves the main sequence. According to calculations by Dr. Kasting, the sun will have increased in luminosity by about 10 percent 1.1 billion years from now. That may be enough to initiate rapid water loss. If by then Earth has insufficient cloud cover to protect it from some of the sun's glare, water will evaporate at a rapid rate, rising as vapor into the stratosphere. At high altitude, solar radiation will split water molecules into oxygen and hydrogen, and the hydrogen will rapidly escape into space.

But long before then Earth may be experiencing catastrophic distress. One possibility is that about 100 million years from now, rising terrestrial temperatures will speed the weathering of Earth's rocks. This, according to Dr. James E. Lovelock, a British environmental scientist, will remove carbon dioxide from the atmosphere and convert it into carbonate compounds. By lowering atmospheric carbon dioxide, a greenhouse effect may be reduced, but most of the world's plants, except for corn, sugar and a few others, will be starved of their main nutrient.

After 11 billion years on the main sequence, the sun will change course. At first it will cool somewhat, but soon afterward, it will turn into a branch of the Hertzsprung-Russell Diagram in which it begins its evolution as a red giant.

As the hydrogen supply of the sun is exhausted, a point will come at which the helium in its core, which is produced by hydrogen fusion, will also ignite. By a thermonuclear process, helium atoms will fuse to become carbon and oxygen.

At first, Dr. Boothroyd said, as helium fusion in its core begins, the sun will become somewhat less luminous and will slip part of the way back from its status as a red giant. But as the helium in the core is used up, the sun will resume its climb into red-gianthood, eventually experiencing a half-dozen explosive ignitions of fusion in the outer helium shell of the star. These blasts are expected to blow much of the sun's mass into space.

Finally, some 12.4 billion years after the sun was born, it will undergo the last of its spasmodic helium flashes, and with its thermonuclear fuel practically gone, the dying star will form a planetary nebula, a small, hot stellar remnant surrounded by a large cloud of greenish incandescent gas. Further cooling will leave the sun as a white dwarf, consisting of matter so dense that one cubic inch would weigh about 10 tons. At the end of the trail, the sun will become a black dwarf orbited by the cinders of its former planetary system, including the frozen remnant of the long lifeless Earth.

There Earth will continue to spin, perhaps forever.

"Fortunately, we still have lots and lots of time," Dr. Boothroyd said.

—MALCOLM W. BROWNE, September 1994

7

THE
LATEST FROM
THE FIELD

Natural disasters will never cease, unless the Earth should become a dead planet, bereft of climatic or geological change. Earthquakes, volcanoes and hurricanes are titanic forces far too powerful to be tamed. But with increasing knowledge, scientists can hope to give enough warning to avert calamity.

Unfortunately the warning system that now works so well for hurricanes, saving maybe thousands of lives every year, has no reliable counterpart as regards earthquakes or volcanoes. Popacatepetl, a volcano that could threaten much of Mexico City, is an ever-present menace, sullen, intractable and largely unpredictable, although experts did recently succeed in forecasting a major eruption.

Also hard to forecast are the droughts that periodically threaten the Midwest and other regions. Drought causes as much economic damage as floods and hurricanes combined. Tree rings tell a depressing story of droughts that lasted for decades or even a century.

But not everything is gloomy. Scientists feel they are getting a better handle on understanding the genesis of lightning strikes. And one kind of disaster, the cloud of carbon dioxide that erupted from Lake Nyos in Cameroon, may be susceptible to a fairly simple fix, a deep pipe that lets the lake blow off surplus gas before it becomes a hazard.

—NICHOLAS WADE

Watchful Eyes on a Violent Giant

POPOCATEPETL, MEXICO'S MAGNIFICENT AND MYSTICAL 17,945-foot peak, has been called the world's most dangerous volcano. Nearly 30 million people live within view of it, most of them in Mexico City, 40 miles west, and Puebla, 30 miles east. More than 300,000 people living in the danger zone directly under the volcano regard it as a living thing, a magical man-mountain, a geological god giving rain and rich land. On Dec. 18, 2000, when it erupted in what some scientists said was its biggest explosion in a millennium, they came to regard it with a little more fear than awe.

But they now have more than a little science to mix with their magic. Since 1994, when it awakened from a seven-decade slumber, Popocatepetl (which is pronounced poh-poh-kah-TEH-peh-til and means "smoking mountain" in Nahuatl, the indigenous language of Mexico) has become the world's most elaborately monitored volcano. Seismologists, geologists, volcanologists and mathematicians have been watching and recording its every tremor. As a result, scientists were able to predict within hours that it was about to blow on Dec. 18, and officials evacuated more than half of the people in the valleys below.

And therein lies a tale.

On average, a volcano erupts somewhere about once a week. Ten or 12 eruptions a year have the potential to kill people. Two or three a decade threaten mass death and destruction. And 75 percent of the biggest eruptions in the past two centuries came from volcanoes never known, in human history, to have erupted before.

Scientists understand a lot about volcanoes. They know the Earth has three layers: its dense core, its partly molten mantle, and its crust, broken into 16 major tectonic plates, moving almost imperceptibly, a few inches a year.

And they know that all along the Pacific coast, from Alaska to Chile, the plates that underlie the ocean are scraping under the land. At the edges of these plates, rivers of molten rock, called magma, bubble toward the surface of the Earth. Magma that reaches the surface is called lava, and volcanoes are built from accumulated lava, rock, ash and dust. In hot spots along rifts in the plates, the magma can erupt with tremendous force.

But there is much scientists do not know about why volcanoes erupt when they do, and as a result volcanoes remain a lethal threat to those who live around them.

Since May 18, 1980, when Mount St. Helens erupted in Washington State, causing 57 deaths, volcanoes have killed nearly 30,000 people, driven more than one million people from their homes, and caused billions of dollars of damage. More than 25,000 people were killed in 1985, when the Nevado del Ruiz volcano in Colombia erupted after months of restless rumbling, sending rivers of mud and ash called lahars down on the town of Armero.

The deaths could have been prevented, scientists say, if the volcano's warning signs could have been detected, analyzed and transmitted in time.

Volcano monitoring systems do exist. After Mount St. Helens, scientists from the United States Geological Survey began devising portable volcano monitoring instruments that could be set up together in 70-pound early-warning systems. They could chart changes in sulphur dioxide and carbon dioxide in the air, the tilt and temperature of the ground, the most minor earthquakes and tremors, and debris flows that would otherwise go undetected. Transmitters to send the data—with radio, antenna and a year's power supply—were packed into nine-gallon steel drums. The system provided a continuous, real-time history of seismic activity.

The system was originally intended for the Pacific Coast ranges of California, Oregon and Washington, but after Nevado del Ruiz, the United States Office of Foreign Disaster Assistance, an arm of the Agency for International Development, asked the geological survey to set up a global program. The result was the world's only rapid-response team of its kind, the Volcano Disaster Assistance Program.

"The truth of the matter with volcanoes is that no one knows what will happen next," said Dan Miller, a research geologist who is the chief of the program, which has headquarters in Vancouver, Wash. "Volcanoes are not that consistent and not that well understood. But what happened at Nevado del Ruiz didn't need to have happened."

When a volcano becomes active, the team can move quickly (though only when invited by another nation's government, through a formal request to the State Department). It now has worked at 19 volcanoes in 15 nations. Within days, it can install monitoring equipment, detect magma flowing to the surface and forecast eruptions with reasonable accuracy.

"Forecasting exactly when an eruption will occur is very difficult," Dr. Miller said. "And eruptions can go on for months and even years."

When Mount Pinatubo in the Philippines reawakened on April 2, 1991, after lying dormant for more than 500 years, Philippine scientists called in the disaster assistance program to install a monitoring network. The sensors gave clear warning of a catastrophic explosion, which came two months later. By that time, 75,000 people, including 18,000 members of the American military, had been evacuated.

"We were lucky," Dr. Miller said. "The volcano was threatening big, destructive eruptions and it produced them a few days after the signs were clear and accurately interpreted. Tens of thousands of lives were saved. And the entire effort cost less than $1.5 million."

Things went less well at Montserrat, in the British West Indies, in 1995. The team installed its monitoring network at the Soufriere volcano, watched magma moving up to surface and transmitted the danger signs. But it was more than two years before the volcano truly exploded, by which time the force of the warnings had dwindled. At least 19 people died and the capital, Plymouth, was destroyed by lava and ash.

In December 1994, Popocatepetl, which is geologically similar to the volcanoes in the Cascade Range in Washington and Oregon that the United States geological team knew best, became active with a series of eruptions after lying dormant since 1927.

Scientists from the National University of Mexico and the National Disaster Prevention Center (known by its Spanish acronym, Cenapred) already had installed four seismic sensing stations on the volcano's flanks. But they asked for help. The result has been, by most volcanologists' accounts, one of the world's best volcano monitoring networks.

Working together, the Mexican and United States scientists set up a device called a tiltmeter to detect infinitesimal shifts in the slope of the volcano, which becomes swollen when magma rises into it. A tiltmeter works like a carpenter's level, with a bubble in the middle that sets off an electrical impulse when it shifts. The one at Popocatepetl is so sensitive that if you had a 3,000-foot bar of steel, and slipped a nickel under one end, the tiltmeter at the other end would detect it.

The Mexicans and the United States team installed a special seismometer, an acoustic-flow monitor, that could pick up a small lahar flowing by. They had specially equipped surveyors' rods, enhanced by lasers, to detect bulges in the volcano.

They deployed other sensors to pick up ground movements along with shifts in gases, electrical and magnetic fields that flow from subterranean movements of magma. They had special detectors to listen for the phenomena called harmonic tremors, Earth vibrations set off by moving magma for reasons no one really understands. They also had, it should go without saying, a network of Popocams, or video cameras hooked up to the Internet, watching over the smoking mountain.

Earthworm, which allows instant acquisition and sharing of data over the Internet. Two weeks ago, as the volcano began showing signs of a big eruption, Cenapred scientists could sit in a control room on the southern edge of Mexico City and watch it.

"These guys are operating at the state of the art," said Jim Luhr, director of the Smithsonian Institution's Global Volcanism Program.

But their work would mean nothing if the people who live under the volcano did not get their message or ignored it.

When a warning goes from Cenapred through radio and television it reaches most of the 217 towns in the danger zone within minutes. And in the 24 towns that radio cannot reach, a satellite telephone alerts local leaders, who ring church bells to sound the alarm.

Alejandro Rivera Dominguez, a seismologist affiliated with the Center for Disaster Prevention at Puebla University, described the 300,000 people around Popocatepetl as mostly poor, many of them farmers who are especially reluctant to leave their fields and herds behind. To them, he said, the volcano is a sacred symbol that cannot be fathomed by science, a rain god and a giver of good harvests.

The authorities, he said, have learned to speak and think of Popocatepetl with a more folkloric, more magical language in order to better communicate warnings to the villagers, Mr. Rivera said.

That may be. For nearly a week before Popocatepetl's spectacular nighttime explosion on Dec. 18, the alarms had gone out from Cenapred to the countryside, the church bells had rung. Thousands heeded the warnings, but thousands resisted, saying they were less fearful of lava and ash than the possibility that soldiers and policemen sent to protect them would loot their homes instead.

"We've been holding out for a week now," said Jose Felipe Pacheco, 26, a farmer from Santiago Xanitzintla, one of the communities closest to the crater, as he left his home reluctantly, under pressure from army officers, more than eight hours after the first huge eruption. "Our belongings, all that we have, and have earned through such sacrifice—and to think that we could come back to an empty home, losing everything you've worked for.

"Leaving is in my best interest," he said. "But staying is also in my best interest."

—TIM WEINER, January 2001

Persistent and Severe, Drought Strikes Again

TORNADOES, HURRICANES AND FLOODS are the stuff of television drama; they make people sit up and take notice. Not so with drought. It is a far more subtle weather catastrophe that "sneaks up on you" and consequently commands little awe or respect, says Dr. Donald A. Wilhite, a Nebraska climatologist who is an expert on the subject. He calls it the Rodney Dangerfield of natural disasters.

Although it might not stir the emotions, in an average year drought is responsible for about as much economic damage as floods and hurricanes combined. Nor is it a rare phenomenon, as many people erroneously believe. Instead, it is a persistent and permanent feature of weather and climate, severely affecting some part of the United States almost every year.

So it is that in 2000, much of the country's midsection and a broad swath of its southern tier from Arizona to Florida—roughly a quarter of the territory of the contiguous 48 states in all—is already experiencing a moderate to severe drought with the peak months for drought still ahead. If long-range forecasts of below-normal rainfall and above-normal temperatures are accurate, conditions may well get worse.

As a new growing season begins in the Iowa-Nebraska-Illinois breadbasket, severe deficiencies of soil moisture are creating a potential new threat to farmers' chronically sagging fortunes. The water level of the Great Lakes is approaching all-time lows; not since 1965 have Lakes Michigan and Huron been so low. The prospect looms of huge financial losses in agriculture and recreation. And as always, drought raises the risk of wildfires.

So experts are plumbing the past and investigating today's changing climate as part of an effort to understand drought better and to gauge whether longer and more severe droughts may lie ahead.

For instance, could another Dust Bowl or an even worse drought be in the nation's future? Based on scientists' analyses of tree rings, ancient soils and other evidence, the answer is almost certainly yes. Many experts believe that with the world's climate warming as it is, droughts will become more frequent and severe. But apart from that, and regardless of whether humans are responsible for global warming, there is plenty of evidence that big, damaging droughts are inevitable. The only question is when they will come.

A 1998 study by federal scientists, for instance, found that droughts as widespread and severe as that of the Dust Bowl of the 1930's, when 65 percent of the country was affected at the drought's peak in 1934, have occurred once or twice a century over the last 300 to 400 years. A decade-long drought, the study found, occurs about once every 500 years.

More recent analyses of tree-ring data have identified a 16th-century megadrought that affected much of the continent for years, far outstripping any drought of the 20th century in persistence and severity. It was during this drought that the first English colony in America, at Roanoke Island in North Carolina, disappeared, and experts now believe the drought is what killed it off.

The report, by Dr. David W. Stahle, a tree-ring analyst at the University of Arkansas, Dr. Edward R. Cook, an analyst of ancient climates at the Lamont-Doherty Earth Observatory of Columbia University, and six colleagues, appeared in the March 21 issue of *Eos*, a scientific publication of the American Geophysical Union.

Megadroughts lasting a century or two are known to have occurred in what is now California over the last 3,500 years. Droughts of similar severity have also been implicated in the downfall of the empire of the Maya in Central America a millennium ago; the Akkadian empire (the world's first) in Mesopotamia 4,200 years ago (that drought lasted 300 years) and several pre-Inca cultures in South America.

But it does not take a megadrought to bring disaster, and the emerging record of past dry spells contains several smaller ones that would surely devastate much of the United States if they materialized again. In the 20th century, major droughts in the 1950's and in 1988 were second only to the Dust Bowl. The tree-ring studies showed that comparable droughts materialized in the 1750's, 1820's, 1850's and 1860's.

The worst drought in recent years came in the summer of 1988, when a combination of intense heat and widespread moisture deficiency baked more than a third of the country for weeks. It destroyed at least half the crops on the Great Plains, lowered water levels in the Mississippi River so much that barges ran aground and created the conditions for a summer-long run of forest fires in the West. The most famous engulfed great swatches of Yellowstone National Park in that area's biggest conflagration in at least 200 years.

All of this makes it abundantly clear that drought is a standard feature of climate, not an exception to the rule.

But disaster planners often do not see it that way, and consequently pay more attention to other threats like floods, says Dr. Wilhite, who directs the National Drought Mitigation Center, a research and planning organization at the University of Nebraska.

If that is so, one reason may be that drought is rarely a cause of death or destruction of buildings, although drought-associated heat waves often send mortality temporarily skyrocketing. (Summer heat makes drought worse by speeding evaporation of moisture; and when there is no more moisture to evaporate, the sun's energy goes entirely into heating the land, which in turn makes the air above it even hotter.)

Another possible reason for a relative lack of urgency about drought is that it is a creeping phenomenon. "It's hard to know when you're in a drought," Dr. Wilhite said. "When do you ring the bell?" As things stand now, he said, people "essentially don't become aware of drought and the dimensions of its impact until they're in the middle of it; at that point, there's not a lot you can do about it."

According to figures compiled by Dr. Wilhite's organization, drought costs the nation $6 billion to $8 billion a year on average, compared with $2.4 billion for floods and $1.2 billion to $4.8 billion for hurricanes. The worst droughts easily outstrip the worst floods and hurricanes; for instance, the 1988 drought exacted a toll of about $40 billion, while the Mississippi Valley floods of 1993, the worst of the century, cost $28 billion at most, and Hurricane Andrew in 1992, the most expensive on record, caused $25 billion to $33 billion in damages.

Damages might be reduced by better planning, Dr. Wilhite said. For example, farmers might switch to drought-resistant crops, and water conservation measures could be planned before a drought occurred instead of in a crisis.

Soil management and tillage practices have improved since the Dust Bowl days, when vast expanses of topsoil simply dried up and blew away, and to some extent the improvements might ease the impact of a comparable drought today, he said. But "some things you can't do anything about," he said, including depletion of aquifers and the dropping of water levels in reservoirs, lakes, rivers and streams.

What does the future hold?

Over the last 25 years, the Earth's average surface temperature has risen at a rate equal to about 3.5 degrees per century. Mainstream scientists believe it will continue to rise at that rate in the 21st century if emissions of heat-trapping waste industrial gases like carbon dioxide are not reduced.

A warming atmosphere has two effects related to precipitation, experts say: it causes more moisture to evaporate from the oceans and fresh waters, thus producing heavier rains. Scientists at the National Climatic Data Center in Asheville, N.C., have detected a clear trend in that direction.

But when it does not rain for a long time, a warmer atmosphere also intensifies drought by making more moisture evaporate from the land, faster. No trend toward increased drought has been detected over the last century, said Dr. David R. Easterling, a researcher at the Climatic Data Center. But he said that eventually, in the interior of the continent, drought could win out over increasing precipitation if the atmosphere warmed enough.

Global warming could also affect the size and frequency of forest fires. A recent study of charcoal layers in Yellowstone, reflecting the last 17,000 years of fire history there, found that the number of fires peaked before 7,000 years ago, a time when summers were warmer than now.

The implication is that while fires would become more frequent in a warmer climate, they would also become smaller because less fuel, in the form of dead trees and forest litter, would have a chance to build up, said Dr. Cathy Whitlock, a geographer at the University of Oregon who was a co-author of the study. The other authors, also at Oregon, were Dr. Sarah H. Millspaugh and Dr. Patrick J. Bartlein. The paper appeared in March in the journal *Geology*.

A longtime expert on wildfire in the West, Dr. William Romme of Fort

Lewis College in Durango, Colo., said the study suggested that "if the warming trend over the last century continues, as it appears it will, we can expect some really dramatic changes in fire behavior." It is likely, he said, that more frequent fires will allow less fuel to build up, in time making big conflagrations like that of 1988 less probable.

As for drought itself, some scientists believe, the frequency and severity of future dry spells could increase as a result of natural, periodic oscillations in Pacific Ocean surface temperatures on a scale of decades. The Stahle-Cook paper in *Eos* suggests that the 16th-century megadrought could have been caused by a prolonged cooling phase in some areas of the Pacific.

Back-and-forth oscillations in the Pacific temperatures alter atmospheric circulation patterns that deliver moisture to North America. One phase, which favors development of the phenomenon known as La Nina, is associated with drought in much of the United States. That phase has prevailed for the last two years—La Nina years—and some scientists predict that it will predominate in the decades just ahead.

For that matter, Dr. Easterling said, the big drought of 1988 was "pretty well tied" to La Nina. So was last summer's severe drought in the Middle Atlantic region and Northeast, many scientists believe. And so is this year's developing drought across the southern tier and midsection.

So far, the drought of 2000 has been most clearly manifest in the Great Lakes region. A combination of lower precipitation and high temperatures over the last three years, coupled with relatively little snow, has reduced stream flows in the region to well below normal.

In the lakes themselves, there has been "an unprecedented drop" in water levels over the last two to three years, said Dr. Frank H. Quinn, senior research hydrologist for the National Oceanic and Atmospheric Administration's Great Lakes Environmental Research Laboratory in Ann Arbor, Michigan. Lakes Huron and Michigan, which are really one body of water, have dropped about three feet, the biggest such drop in 140 years of record keeping, ending a 30-year run of above-average levels.

This has some benefits: "We will have the best beaches in 35 years and considerably less erosion," Dr. Quinn said. But in a region whose economy is in so many ways tied to the lakes, he said, there will also be large negative effects: the region's billion-dollar water recreation industry is likely to be hit hard, as many marinas no longer have enough water to hold boats. Lake freighters will not be able to load to full capacity. Less forceful water flows will reduce hydropower production downstream of the lakes.

The drought has not yet really pinched the midcontinent agricultural regions, since the growing season is only beginning, Dr. Wilhite said. Nor have the high evaporation levels of late spring and summer set in, not to mention the normal summertime increase in demand for water. The squeeze is likely to come, Dr. Wilhite said, if and when long-range forecasts of abnormal warmth and dryness materialize in the next three months.

The most recent observations show that much of the southern tier from Arizona to Florida is also in a severe drought, but the latest forecasts call for normal rainfall in most of that swath over the next three months.

But the forecasts can and do change from month to month. So for those in the dry regions, it is a time to prepare, watch and wait.

—WILLIAM K. STEVENS, April 2000

Lightning's Shocking Secrets; Clues to Tornadoes and Other Mysteries

IF ZEUS WERE ALIVE and chucking lightning bolts down from the sky, he would be perched right over Goodland, Kan. That is where many of the nation's most violent thunderstorms are spawned, the kind that drop baseball-size hail, tornadoes, torrents of rain and furious winds across the Great Plains states.

So when scientists from nearly a dozen universities and government laboratories recently decided to carry out an advanced study on what causes lightning and severe weather, they deployed their instruments on the cornfields around Goodland, hunkered down and waited for Zeus to rock and roll.

Their eight-week experiment, called the Severe Thunderstorm Electrification and Precipitation Study, or Steps, ended on Sunday. Scientists say that the experiment turned up some stunning surprises that may force them to revise their theories of how lightning is produced.

Among the discoveries were many instances of a rare kind of so-called reverse lightning, in which electrons shoot upward from the ground to the cloud, instead of downward as in normal lightning, and new clues about what causes strange lights called blue jets, red sprites, elves and trolls that appear in the upper atmosphere above thunderstorms. Sprites, which last long enough to be seen with the naked eye, happen only above reverse, or "positive cloud to ground" lightning, adding to the mystery of both phenomena.

Most important, researchers witnessed several events within severe storms that seemed to predict when tornadoes would form. For example, they observed updraft regions in clouds where all lightning suddenly ceased. Moments later, tornadoes formed in that area. If lightning-free

208

zones usually precede tornadoes, they said, weather forecasters might be able to watch for these "electrical holes" in the clouds and make better short-term predictions for severe weather, including large hail, heavy rain and tornadoes.

The study was organized because the details of precipitation, hail and lightning formation within severe storms are still not completely understood, said Dr. Morris Weisman, a scientist with the National Center for Atmospheric Research in Boulder, Colorado, who helped coordinate each day's observations.

"Given similar initial weather conditions, we don't know why some storms produce downpours while others contain just as much water vapor but make very little or no rain," Dr. Weisman said.

With financing from the National Science Foundation, the scientists converged on Goodland armed with radar, weather balloons, mini-weather stations on wheels, lightning detectors and an airplane that could fly into the heart of thunderstorms.

They set up this equipment along the Kansas-Colorado border, where moist air from the Gulf of Mexico meets hot, dry air from the Southwest to cook up storms so huge they can last for days as they move east.

Scientists have thought for years that they understood basically what happens inside storm clouds, said Dr. Donald MacGorman of the National Severe Storms Laboratory in Norman, Okla. For example, lightning is generated in cold upper layers of air when particles of partly frozen water and ice crystals collide inside large clouds. These collisions generate positive and negative electrical charges the same way that walking across a carpet on a dry day can build up static charges and result in a shock when a person touches a doorknob.

In general, negative charges sink to the middle or lower parts of the cloud, while positive charges rise to upper levels, he said. When air can no longer insulate these opposite charges, an avalanche of runaway electrons initiates a lighting bolt. Most electrical discharges move sideways within or between clouds, but electrical charges can also flow to the ground in familiar flashes of lightning.

As for storms, as hot air near the ground rises into cooler regions, any moisture in the air condenses into cloud droplets. Strong updrafts promote the formation of rain, which can fall and drag air masses back down to the surface. Storms like this are short-lived. But if winds are strong or if there are significant temperature differences and large amounts of moisture, very large clouds can evolve into thunderheads that acquire a vortex of circulating air. These super cells can produce tornadoes and other violent weather.

But, as everyone knows, weather is fickle, Dr. MacGorman said. Some supercells produce rain, lightning, hail and tornadoes; some produce no rain or lightning but pound crops with large hail; others produce floods and tornadoes but no lightning and hail. The reasons for such different outcomes will eventually be found in the minute physical properties of storm clouds and a better understanding of chaotic systems, Dr. MacGorman said.

For the last two months, the Steps investigators met every morning at the National Weather Service center in Goodland and pored over weather data, looking for the storms.

On good days, when the weather was bad, the scientists scrambled into action. Dr. Erik Rasmussen, a scientist with the Severe Storms Laboratory, sent out a crew to chase storms in six Oldsmobiles fitted with ski racks mounted with weather instruments. These volunteers collected data once a second on winds, temperature, pressure and humidity under and near the storm front. Conditions measured on the ground might help researchers learn what is happening in the clouds overhead.

For example, on June 29 the volunteers discovered that the air falling to the ground along the rear flank of a very large storm had suddenly turned warm. Minutes later, the storm spawned quarter-size hail and a tornado. Still later, measuring other downdrafts at the back of the same storm, they found that the falling air had suddenly turned cold. Minutes later it rained and hailed but no tornado formed.

While this was going on, Charlie Summers, a pilot employed by the South Dakota School of Mines and Technology, took to the skies in a single-engine airplane designed to fly through severe weather. Resembling a 1940's Studebaker with wings, the craft is armored with 700 pounds of aluminum coating, a metal grate to keep hailstones out of its carburetor and thick acrylic windshields.

Strapped into a four-way harness, Mr. Summers flew the plane into the heart of severe storms where he was buffeted by 50-mile-an-hour vertical winds, direct lightning strikes, hail and enough ice to temporarily stall the engine. Instruments measured the spectrum of water and ice particles in the clouds, air pressure, temperature and electric fields.

The airplane conked out about a week before the experiment ended, said Dr. Andrew Detwiler, an expert on storm electrification at the South Dakota School. But the aircraft gathered large amounts of data that will be compared with information collected on the ground, he said.

While Mr. Summers flew, other scientists operated special radar stations that could directly measure the size and shape of water particles in every cloud. Conventional radar cannot do this. The added information is expected to shed light on exactly how lightning is generated.

To study lightning, scientists from the New Mexico School of Mines and Technology in Socorro turned on 13 specially built lightning detectors that were laid out in cornfields under radar observation. Each detector is about the size of a small coffee table and contains a receiver that measures how long it takes for radio signals, which are always produced by lightning strikes, to arrive, allowing researchers to calculate the exact time and location of every lightning strike in every storm that occurred during the experiment.

By comparing this detailed picture of where lightning occurs with radar images and airplane data on precipitation, it may be possible to learn more about how lightning is generated, said Dr. Paul Krehbiel, who helped develop the system.

Preliminary data show that charge fields—the layers of positively and negatively charged particles within clouds—do not fall into the conventional pattern, Dr. Krehbiel said. They are often upside down, meaning negative on top and positive below.

This inverted polarity was also observed by scientists from the National Severe Storms Laboratory, who released up to four weather balloons into the belly of each storm. Each balloon measured temperatures, humidity, pressures, wind directions and electric fields.

A surprising number of storms produced the reversed, "positive cloud-to-ground" lightning that was thought to be restricted to very large supercell storms, said Dr. David Rust, chief of the Mesoscale Research and Applications Division at the Severe Storms Laboratory. "We're seeing it in ordinary smaller storms" along with electrically inverted charge fields, he said.

In a positive-to-ground lightning strike, positive charges first rush from the cloud to the ground, creating a lightning channel through which electrons flow from the ground back up to the cloud. Such lightning strikes tend to carry more charge, last tens of seconds longer and be less branched than the more common negative-to-ground lightning. But how this reversal of charge occurs remains something of a mystery, Dr. Rust said.

"Storms may reverse their polarity all the time, but we just never knew it," Dr. Krehbiel said. While scientists on the ground and in the air over Kansas and Colorado ran around collecting information on each storm, other Steps researchers sat quietly at an observation post called the Yucca Ridge Field Station in the foothills of the Rockies near Fort Collins, Colorado.

There, with an unobstructed view of the Great Plains, researchers waited for blue jets, red sprites, elves and trolls—strange lights that could be seen with the naked eye or detected with instruments over the tops of thunderstorms to the east.

Blue jets are extremely energetic fields of charged particles that rise up to 30 miles from the tops of clouds. After they occur, lightning stops for several seconds. Red sprites are striated glowing ribbons that rise high above the jets and reach the ionosphere, lasting for 3 to 10 milliseconds. They happen only over regions of reverse lightning. Elves are thin, expanding doughnuts of light found on the lower edge of the ionosphere. They tend to occur above sprites after a lightning pulse. Trolls are propagating waves of energy that appear to come back out of cloud tops and hook up with sprites, but no one really knows what they are.

"If we were biologists, it would be like we discovered some new body parts," said Dr. Walt Lyons, a scientist with FMA Research, a company that runs Yucca Ridge. Somehow, he explained, lightning discharges in the lower atmosphere are having effects in the upper atmosphere.

During the experiment, Dr. Lyons and his colleagues observed more than 1,000 red sprites over the dissipating regions of storms where clouds flattened out and produced a type of horizontal discharge called spider lightning or creepy-crawly lightning. These clouds also produced reverse lightning over which the sprites were seen.

"We're happy but exhausted," Dr. Lyons said. It will take time to analyze what happened inside those clouds, he said, but whatever is going on may help explain sprites.

Indeed, each researcher said it will take many years to analyze all the data collected on the Great Plains this spring and summer.

—SANDRA BLAKESLEE, July 2000

Trying to Tame
the Roar of Deadly Lakes

ON THE EVENING OF AUG. 21, 1986, a cloud of carbon dioxide erupted from Lake Nyos in the mountainous region of northwestern Cameroon. Heavy and deadly, the gas rolled down hills, into valleys and villages, suffocating everything in its path. By the next morning, 1,700 people were dead.

Because of that eruption, and a 1984 emission at Lake Monoun 59 miles to the southeast, the people of the region have lived with the fear that these lakes will kill again. Indeed, both lakes contain more lethal gas than they did before the eruptions.

But now, an international team of scientists has taken the first steps to disarm the killer lakes.

By lowering a polyethylene pipe into the depths of Lake Nyos, the scientists have allowed gas-rich water at the bottom of the lake to froth up in a great fountain. The carbon dioxide, generated by volcanic activity deep in the Earth, can now escape harmlessly into the atmosphere rather than building up under pressure and, ultimately, exploding.

"This will be the first time we will have been able to prevent a natural disaster," said Dr. James G. Smith, a geoscience adviser at the federal Agency for International Development, which paid for most of the effort. He called it "truly amazing."

In addition to placing the first of what the scientists hope will be a series of de-gassing pipes, they have installed an early warning system on each lake. If levels of carbon dioxide rise, sirens and strobes will go off and people in the region can try to escape.

"The Nyos people seem very happy," Dr. Gregory Tanyileke of the Cameroonian Institute for Geological and Mining Research said from a satellite phone at the lake shore. "It is the end of a nightmare for them."

Although scientists are pleased so far, they note that the danger is far from over. Lake Nyos still contains enormous amounts of carbon dioxide, and one pipe alone will not be enough to remove it.

The team would like to put four or five more pipes in Nyos to eliminate the hazard there and to install pipes in Monoun, which remains extremely dangerous. Team members estimate that they need $2 million, but they have no immediate money source.

Lake Nyos and Lake Monoun are crater lakes, formed as cooled volcanic craters filled with water. In most such lakes, any gas that enters from underground sources eventually reaches the atmosphere when layers of water in the lakes periodically mix from top to bottom or turn over, said Dr. George W. Kling, a University of Michigan biologist who has studied Nyos and Monoun and is one of the leaders of the de-gassing team.

But these two lakes, along with Lake Kivu in East Africa, which has not erupted, are unusual. The boundary, called the chemocline, between the deep water, rich with gas and minerals, and the fresh upper water stays intact. Gas saturates the bottom water and stays trapped there, like the carbon dioxide in a sealed bottle of seltzer.

Then something—perhaps a strong wind, cool weather, a storm or a landslide—causes a pocket of upper water to sink. That movement, in turn, provokes some bottom water to rise. Without the weight of the water above to contain it, the gas comes out of solution, like the bubbles that emerge when a seltzer bottle is opened.

In the case of Lake Nyos in 1986, the jet of gas and water shot up about 260 feet, Dr. Kling said. Moving at about 45 miles an hour, the gas reached villages 12 miles away. The lake released about a cubic kilometer of carbon dioxide—about 10 football stadiums full, from the field to the top of the bleachers, Dr. Kling said. At Lake Monoun, the cloud was much smaller, but still deadly. It killed 37 people as they walked to work early one morning.

The 672-foot pipe installed last month in Lake Nyos takes some of the pressure off. It spews a jet of gas and water that rises as high as 165 feet. Over the course of a year, it will release about 706 million cubic feet of gas, said Dr. Michel Halbwachs of the University of Savoy in France, who directed the installation and led an initial de-gassing test in 1995.

That amount of gas is about three or four times as much as is thought to enter the lake in that time, said Dr. Kling. Lake Nyos contains 10.6 billion cubic feet to 14.1 billion cubic feet of carbon dioxide — 16,000 times the amount in an average lake, he added.

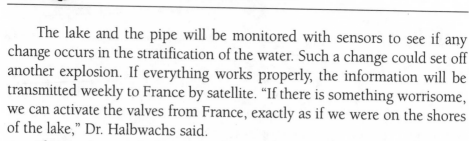

The lake and the pipe will be monitored with sensors to see if any change occurs in the stratification of the water. Such a change could set off another explosion. If everything works properly, the information will be transmitted weekly to France by satellite. "If there is something worrisome, we can activate the valves from France, exactly as if we were on the shores of the lake," Dr. Halbwachs said.

Those valves are high up in the pipe, and can open to allow water that is less gaseous to enter the column. This influx of more stable, less gaseous water reduces the force of the fountain and, if all valves are opened, stops the flow altogether. Once Cameroonian researchers have been fully trained, they will do all the monitoring and control from a lakeside observatory and science center that is under construction.

Although the scientists who have worked on this problem for many years say they are pleased with the success of the first pipe, they remain worried.

The CO_2 sirens, which are used on volcanoes around the world because they emit deadly gases, will help. "But in terms of mitigating all the danger to the people around the lake, I don't feel good about it," said William C. Evans, a chemist with the United States Geological Survey who would like to see more pipes installed in Nyos soon.

In addition to the pent-up carbon dioxide, Nyos contains another hazard that has not been tackled: a weak dam at its northern edge. If the dam ruptured, it could cause a gas eruption and a flood that could flow as far as Nigeria, drowning or displacing up to 10,000 people.

"I am now a bit more concerned about that erosion than about the gas," said Umaru Sule, who survived the Nyos disaster but lost most of his family, and who now lives in Oklahoma, where he just completed his master's in agricultural education. "They should try to maybe see how they could reinforce the dam."

Mr. Sule's concerns may be addressed this spring. Dr. Halbwachs of the University of Savoy said a team of five scientists from a French group called Hydrologists Without Borders was planning to visit Lake Nyos in April to see if the members could do just that.

"So far, so good," said Dr. Tanyileke of the Cameroonian geological institute. "It looks as if some of our dreams are finally coming true."

—MARGUERITE HALLOWAY, February 2001